Preaching About
Family Relationships

Preaching About ... Series

Preaching About Family Relationships

Elizabeth Achtemeier

The Westminster Press
Philadelphia

Scripture quotations from the Revised Standard Version of the Bible are copyrighted 1946, 1952, © 1971, 1973 by the Division of Christian Education of the National Council of the Churches of Christ in the U.S.A. and are used by permission.

The lines of verse in chapter 5 are from *The Family Reunion* by T. S. Eliot, copyright 1939 by T. S. Eliot; renewed 1967 by Esme Valerie Eliot. Reprinted by permission of Harcourt Brace Jovanovich, Inc., and Faber and Faber Ltd.

The lines of verse in chapter 6 are from *The Poems of Gerard Manley Hopkins*, 4th ed. edited by W. H. Gardner and N. H. MacKenzie. Copyright © 1967 by The Society of Jesus. Reprinted by the permission of Oxford University Press, Inc.

Book design by Christine Schueler

First edition

Published by The Westminster Press®
Philadelphia, Pennsylvania

PRINTED IN THE UNITED STATES OF AMERICA

9 8 7 6 5 4 3 2 1

Library of Congress Cataloging-in-Publication Data

Achtemeier, Elizabeth Rice, 1926–
    Preaching about family relationships.

    (Preaching about— series)
    Bibliography: p.
    1. Family—Religious life. 2. Preaching. I. Title.
II. Series.
BV4526.2.A3 1987   251   87-8178
ISBN 0-664-24080-1 (pbk.)

In gratitude for
that rollicking bunch
of my brothers and their wives
with whom I have always had a ball:

Phil and Irma
Robert and Elaine
Scott and Maurine
Rice

Contents

1

Family Concerns
and the Silence of the Pulpit

The persons in the pews who face us Christian preachers every Sunday morning usually have two principal concerns. They are concerned about their daily work, and they are concerned about their homes and family relationships. Yet, strangely enough, these two concerns are those most often neglected by the pulpit. We sometimes preach about daily work on the Sunday preceding Labor Day. We oftentimes deal with families on Mother's Day or—as the church has renamed it—on the Sunday designated for the Festival of the Christian Home. Otherwise, we are likely to give scant attention in our preaching to these two subjects that most command the interest and thought of our people. Certainly the subjects come up repeatedly in our pastoral relations with our congregations, but we seem to shy away from them in our preaching, as topics too difficult to handle.

Indeed, as far as family relations are concerned, we have largely turned over the guidance of them to the secular culture around us. The experts—the psychologists, therapists, physicians, child guidance counselors, print media, and, yes, even "Dear Abby"—these are the sources to which we look for direction and counsel for our family life. We have learned to utilize invaluable modern psychological methods and insights in the counseling session, but that counseling often is little different from that of any secular practitioner. It rarely is set within the context of the Christian gospel, nor is it often informed by the proclamation from the pulpit of the Word of God for families. We hesitate to preach about home life, and, given the overwhelming importance their homes have in our people's lives, we need to ask why that is so.

One of the principal reasons of course is pastoral. We know the persons facing us there in the pews. We know how many of them are divorced, and how many of their marriages are shaky. We know that Tom Brown's teenage son is using drugs and that Lisa Jones's unmarried daughter just had an abortion. We have agonized with Mary over her struggles as a single parent and with Herbert as the father of an autistic child. We have wept with the lonely widows and with the equally lonely singles. We have baptized these people, confirmed them, married them, comforted and counseled and taught them, stood beside the graves of their loved ones, talked and prayed with them in their homes. In fact, most of our pastoral time has been spent with those among them who have made a shamble of their lives, and somehow it seems improper to discuss their hurts and needs from the pulpit. How can you preach about divorce, for example, when so many in your congregation have gone through that agony? The question is one facing almost every pastor these days.

But perhaps there are other, more subtle reasons why we do not often preach about family concerns, and certainly one of these has to do with our own family life. If we proclaimed from the pulpit God's will for our homes, could we say we practice what we preach? Divorce is becoming rather commonplace among the clergy these days. Every time my husband and I attend a church conference, we hear the news that yet one more minister or seminary teacher has been divorced and is remarried. So do we avoid proclaiming the good news of Christian marriage from the pulpit because our own family failures are all too evident to the eyes and ears of our congregations, or because, most threatening of all, our spouse is sitting out there in the congregation, listening?

We have come up against the problem of the relation of the preacher's own private life to the gospel that he or she preaches, and we are very conscious of the fact that the congregation usually knows how we are raising our kids and perhaps can guess how we are getting along with our mates. So we avoid that topic of home life, which will call our own practice and authority into question.

On the one hand, there is no doubt that our lives must be testimonies to the truth of what we preach. I was a member of a church, some years ago, whose minister preached frequently and very movingly about the necessity of suffering for Christ. But when he began having trouble in his own family, he ducked all necessity of suffering and ran off with the female Sunday school superintendent. Needless to say, the memory of all those sermons became rather distasteful.

On the other hand, does not our hesitancy about preaching on family concerns, because of our own home struggles or difficulties, illumine very clearly the fact that, in the pulpit, we are still trying to be justified by our works? By making our own goodness and our own right family relations the proof of the truth of the gospel, we are saying to our people that the power to be righteous lies in us, and we are thereby denying the gospel of Jesus Christ.

"If I must boast, I will boast of the things that show my weakness," says Paul (2 Cor. 11:30). "[For] we have this treasure in earthen vessels, to show that the transcendent power belongs to God and not to us" (2 Cor. 4:7). That is finally the faith that makes it possible for us to preach on family concerns—and, indeed, on any others. For we affirm with our suffering congregations—affirm with them, rather than standing over against them in phony self-righteousness—that yes, in fact, we do have trouble in our homes. They are beset by conflict and misunderstanding, by weariness and hurt, by trauma and suffering; the best of them know those times. And yet, filtering through the impotency we feel because of our trouble and trials is the transcendent power of God, which carries us and forgives us and saves us, beyond all our power to save ourselves. The Christian preacher who has taken his or her stand firmly in the truth of the gospel need not fear to treat from the pulpit any concern of our sinful human lives.

Such a preacher, further, knows that the Christian God is primarily concerned with those sinful lives. We sometimes make the mistake of thinking that God has to do only with happy homes; we have seen the pictures of too many well-scrubbed, smiling families on the covers of church periodicals. But our Lord told us that he came to call sinners, not the righteous; to minister to those in need of a physician, not the well; and the whole Bible assures us that this God of ours works not only in places of concord and beauty and happiness but also, and first of all, in the darkest corners and most troubled areas of human life. We find God present and at work in brothers' hatred for brother, in the Joseph stories of Genesis. We hear God deciding on an heir to the throne who is the child of murder and adultery, according to the story of David and Solomon. We see God working out his purpose in the siege and sack of Jerusalem, in the prophetic writings. And, yes, we finally see him most fully revealed in the blood and cruelty and indifference of a Roman execution. "He descended into hell"—how true is that affirmation in our creed! The Son of God descends into our evil and our darkness and our death. And because that is so, we know God is present and at work in the midst of the most troubled family, as he is equally at work in the midst of the most serene. It is the preacher's calling to point to that ubiquitous working.

Our hesitancy to preach about family concerns may stem from another fact, however, and perhaps this is the most serious of all: our loss of respect for the biblical authority in relation to home and family. Many preachers carry around with them the unspoken but firm belief that the scriptures no longer have much to say to twentieth-century homes. After all, goes the reasoning, the scriptures reflect the mores and views of societies far removed in time and space from our own, and therefore it would seem to be an anachronistic and misguided exercise to try to impose the family ideals and customs of the ancient Near East on modern American homes. The result is that the Bible's abundant teachings regarding family concerns have been discarded by many preachers as useless and have been replaced with the various positions and opinions found in our modern culture.

Certainly the Bible's views with regard to marriage and home form a striking contrast to those of our society. As Paul said, our message is veiled and unknown to the world (2 Cor. 4:1–4), a stumbling block and foolishness (1 Cor. 1:23), and when the teachings of the Bible are contrasted with those of modern-day America, the disparity is overwhelming.

For example, throughout the Bible the marital relation is viewed as a lifelong and exclusive commitment. In our culture, it can be a temporary arrangement, designed to fulfill the needs of the partners and easily violated or broken if those needs seem not to be met.

Throughout the scriptures, it is assumed that sexual relations belong only in the context of marital commitment, and fornication and adultery are condemned in the strongest terms in both Old and New Testaments. In contrast, our society no longer worries about the fact that extramarital sex is wrong, but only about the incurable epidemics of genital herpes and AIDS that are spread by it. Often our efforts are bent not toward reforming our society's actions but toward finding new drugs to cure the epidemics. Or, to give another example, our culture does not worry about the fact that teenagers are, in our modern euphemism, more and more "sexually active" but only about protecting their right not to have to tell their parents when they are given birth control devices.

The Bible maintains that God is the Lord of life and that we are always dependent upon him. Our culture asks for the absolute and sovereign right of abortion on demand.

The biblical purpose for human life is the service of God and other human beings. Our culture demands the rights of the absolutized self and the development of individual personhood. Indeed, salvation is defined by our society as the fulfillment of the individual, and human relations and marriages are trampled under-foot if they seem to stand in the way of that fulfillment.

The Bible's witness is that commitment lies at the heart of marriage, as it lies at the heart of all abundant life. Our youth increasingly want to forgo commit-ment for an easy and escapable trial marriage.

The view of both Testaments is that marriage is a good gift of a loving God. The view of some radical women's liberationists is that it is a work of the devil, to be shunned for the joys and greater satisfactions, and sometimes homosexuality, of the "sisterhood."

Our Lord teaches us that those who lose their lives for his sake and the gospel's shall find them. The cry of our society, on every hand, is "Give me my rights!"

At almost every juncture, our society's practices are at odds with the biblical requirements. But the inter-esting phenomenon in relation to our society's separa-tion from the Christian faith is the reaction of some preachers to it: They are not at all sure that the biblical views are correct, or that those views should in any way be authoritative for our living.

After all, they think, the scriptures flatly condemn divorce, but is it all that bad? Are there not many instances when divorce is the good and right course of action, and to deny a couple the right to end their marriage would be a denial of the mercy of Christ? In the case of premarital sex, to be sure, there is not a good word said about it in the scriptures. But are there not many situations in which it is the loving thing to do? And are not our young people justified in using their bodies freely as an expression of their very real care in interpersonal relations? Or surely there is much to be said for abortion on demand. Of course no human beings can claim absolute rights, according to the scriptures. But does not a woman have the right to control her own body? And is that not a valid part of women's liberation?

We are very ambiguous about these questions, and already within the minds of the readers of this book there have been formed a dozen different positions on the proper answers to them. But the real question that finally confronts all of us preachers is, To what extent have our positions been shaped on the basis of the biblical authority? Or is there any sense at all in which the scriptures form the canon for our faith and practice in relation to family concerns? Are we merely giving lip service to the authority of the Bible? Do we merely pretend to proclaim the Word of God from the pulpit each Sunday morning, when in actuality what we are doing is proclaiming the latest findings of the psychologists and sociologists and marriage counselors?

We preachers do not want to appear prudish. The church in the past had a very bad record in its attitude toward sex, for example, and we are trying hard to leave that record behind us. We want to be relevant. We want to be "with it." We feel we must speak in a voice of the twentieth century. But perhaps the first question we all should ask in relation to our preaching is, Do we also want to be faithful—faithful to the will of God revealed in his Son Jesus Christ? That is the basic question that must always be posed to us preachers and to all Christians: Are we faithful in our proclamation to our Lord and Savior Jesus Christ?

The scriptures come to us, it must be emphasized, not as a set of legal guidelines, not as a collection of eternal spiritual truths, and certainly not as a volume of proof texts. Rather, the scriptures are handed on to us as a confession of faith and as a witness to the quality and mode of life when it is lived in faithfulness to the Father who has made himself known to us in his Son through the Spirit. Our whole task as preachers, then, is to pass on the confession and the witness. Our task is to preach not ourselves, or our society's ways, but Jesus Christ as Lord, that hearing him our people may trust and, trusting, may be given the power to live abundant and joyful lives of faithfulness to their God.

In the chapters that follow, we shall explore some of the questions we have raised and try to show how we can, in our time, preach about family concerns in faithfulness and integrity.

2

The Social Context
and Its Impact

Any preacher who sets out to deal from the pulpit with a particular topic or issue, such as family concerns, has to have four broad areas of understanding.

First, he or she must thoroughly understand the particular biblical text on which the sermon is based. For every sermon, whether it be topical or doctrinal or expository, should be firmly anchored in a particular text or texts of the scriptures and should grow out of that biblical Word of God. Otherwise the sermon is all too likely to end up proclaiming the preacher's or society's opinions, and those have no transforming power or lasting authority about them.

Second, the preacher must understand how the particular text fits into the context of the Bible as a whole. Otherwise, the one text may be turned into a proof text and laid upon the congregation as a legalistic requirement, with no eye to the broader activity and purpose of God in history, as witnessed to by the scriptures. For example, some preachers may take 1 Corinthians 14:34, "the women should keep silence in the churches," as an absolute command from the apostle Paul and apply it willy-nilly to the females in their congregations, while ignoring completely Paul's equally authoritative words in 1 Corinthians 11, which presuppose that women will pray or prophesy in church services. Or another example: A preacher may

quote Jesus' words concerning divorce in Mark 10:
11–12 but never reflect on their relationship to 2
Corinthians 5:17. We are responsible to the whole
Word of God when we preach, and we must be conscious of the Reformation principle of letting the
scriptures interpret the scriptures. The entire biblical
history of God's saving work, from the call of Abraham
up through the time of the New Testament church,
informs every sermon and sets every individual text in
the context of God's whole self-revelation. Admit-
tedly, it is not easy for a preacher to master that record
of the two thousand years of God's revealing activity,
as it is witnessed to in both Testaments, but preachers
have the responsibility first of all of being interpreters
of the Word of God, and it is assumed that, in that
calling, they will by study and application continually
broaden and deepen their understanding of the Word.

Third, in dealing with a topic like home life, the
preacher must understand the lives of his or her people—their individual biographies, the events they are
experiencing, their hopes and fears, their struggles
and opinions, their reactions to the events of the day,
their progress in their spiritual pilgrimage. The gospel
is meant to be lived by those who hear it preached, and
unless the preacher applies the gospel to the actual
lives of his or her congregation and spells out for them
its implications, they may never hear it and receive it
in their hearts, much less live it in their daily lives.

To be sure, it is finally the Holy Spirit who shines
in our hearts to give us the knowledge of the glory of
God in the face of Jesus Christ. It is finally the Holy
Spirit who awakens faith, and prompts us to trust, and
motivates and empowers us to live the Christian life in
our daily round. Sometimes the Holy Spirit uses the
words of us preachers to do that, sometimes he does
not. But the preacher can do a lot toward clearing
away the obstacles to the working of the Spirit in the
people's hearts. Misunderstandings can be removed,
counterclaims challenged, light thrown on experi-

ences and events, terminologies clarified, applications made clear, implications of the Word spelled out. But all that can be done only by the preacher who knows what his or her congregation is thinking and doing. Pastoral understanding of a congregation goes hand in hand with preaching to them.

Fourth, and so important in dealing with a topic like home life, the preacher must understand the social context of his or her people's lives. We preachers are trying to communicate a gospel that will create Christian family living, but almost every aspect of our American society now militates against that result, and we want to examine that social context of our people's lives in the rest of this chapter.

Perhaps most damaging in our time, our congregations are being subjected to media presentations so massive in their effect that they can legitimately be called brainwashing. Their primary message is that a happy marriage and family life are now obsolete and impossible to achieve. Thus it seems as if the heroine of every television soap opera is divorced or pregnant-out-of-wedlock, and usually both together, and of course the soap opera format has now moved into prime time. Every romantic encounter on the tube is automatically assumed to lead to bed, and whenever some macho hero like J. R. Ewing or James Bond has a new power play to make, he does it with the use of sex. As *TV Guide* once put it in an ad, "The people who write and produce prime-time television have proven their willingness to tackle every imaginable theme over the last decade. . . . They have moved into areas once considered untouchable in prime time. Yet the most common, most crucial of all themes—the capacity of modern men and women to love, trust, share and provide a moral framework for their children—this seems beyond their grasp." Indeed, when one watches many of the top-rated television programs, it becomes rather apparent that their producers and scriptwriters view marriage as an antique and hopeless institution.

And we should never underrate the effect this is having on family life in the United States. As advertisers know and pay dearly for, our lives are shaped and influenced by what comes over the airwaves.

While some movie producers have learned that rousing adventure films or science fiction, with its special effects, can pay off at the box office, many still concentrate on infidelity among midlife, middle-class Americans. Sex clubs, switch groups, homosexuals, and triangles—these often hold Hollywood's rapt attention, and if goodness is found on the human scene, Hollywood is sure it must have come from another planet in the form of E.T. or some equally fanciful figure. Books that do not deliver the most explicit sexuality, in total disregard of family values, rarely find a market on the American publishing scene. Pornography is a booming billion-dollar business, with our children introduced to it at earlier and earlier ages, not only in our movies and books and over cable TV but also in our advertising and in "skin" magazines like *Penthouse.* The American public is being brainwashed—brainwashed by its media—and, given the moral climate that produces, it is little wonder our people get the impression that anything goes.

Thus we regularly hear from the press that a leading politician or military figure of the past carried on an extramarital affair, but that does not dilute the public adulation of such "heroes." Or we are informed that some leading movie stars have had a child together but have no intention of getting married, and that indifference toward family values is accepted as a matter of course.

So much a matter of indifference has the "age of anything goes" become that now, for the first time, the Gallup polling organization reports that the majority of U.S. adults consider premarital sexual relations acceptable (only in the South was this not the case); and this majority is joined even by pastors and theologians, 60 percent of whom consider extramarital sex morally acceptable, according to a 1985 survey conducted by *Psychology Today*. We have wandered a long way from the teaching of our Lord: "For from within, out of the heart of man, come evil thoughts, fornication, theft, murder, adultery. . . . All these evil things come from within, and they defile a man" (Mark 7:21–23 and par.; cf. 1 Cor. 6:9–11).

To believe that all these attitudes and actions do not affect our home life is of course the height of folly, and preachers have ample opportunity to assess the health of American family life merely by reading in newspapers and news magazines the statistical analyses put out by the census bureau or the feature articles highlighting the state of American society.

One out of two marriages in this country now ends in divorce, according to such reports, and despite the fact that 89 percent of all Americans consider their family as one of the most important elements in their life, most of them are not very good at keeping that family intact. Each year 1.1 million children have their homes broken by divorce. The number of families with only one parent grew by 69 percent from 1970 to 1983, and one out of every five children—and more than half of all black children—now live in a one-parent household.[1]

Lest we get bogged down in statistics, however, let us consider just what this means. It means that many children are now the central figure in bitter disputes between their parents over their custody and that some of them are "kidnapped" by the noncustodial parent. It means that the teenagers among them must make the choice of which parent they want to live with—must make that choice when they have no desire to lose either parent. It means that some little ones get shunted back and forth continually between homes and schools, until they no longer know where they live or indeed just who they are. (One national airline has developed a thriving business by designing special package fares and programs for shuttling children back and forth between divorced parents.) It means that most of those children must now adjust to the fact that their father or mother is dating or living with someone else who will eventually replace the absent parent, that the new marriage often brings with it a bewildering array of stepbrothers and stepsisters but that it too is likely to fail, plunging the child into further trauma, further anger and guilt and confusion.

"The trauma of divorce for children," said child psychologist Lee Salk, "is second only to death. Children sense a deep loss and feel they are suddenly vulnerable to forces beyond their control."[2] "No," another expert has countered, "divorce can be even more traumatic than death. The big difference is, death has closure, it's over. With divorce, it's never over."[3] Or, as the head of the Yale Child Study Center put it, "Divorce is one of the most serious and complex mental health crises facing children."[4]

As a result, school systems in some twenty-one states have begun group therapy for children of divorce, in an effort to head off future problems. "At least a third of them are depressed, suffer from low self-esteem, or have behavior problems," said University of Michigan psychologist Neil Kalter.[5] "Children from divorced families are at greater risk of developing these problems." As for the teenagers among them, only about 10 percent "get by with [only] temporary problems in reaction to their parents' divorce," reports adolescent psychiatrist Dr. Allan Z. Schwartzberg,[6] while college students whose parents divorce often find themselves faced with financial problems as well, because tuition money has been used to pay for divorce lawyers. Those "college students experience the same feeling of loss, anger, shame and disillusionment as their younger brothers and sisters . . . at a time when they are trying to assert their independence." Their "studies suffer because of family stress, and coming home for the holidays can be too painful to bear."[7] Little wonder that many of our young people now fear to get married. Better just to play it cool, they think, and live together or remain single, than to get into the morass of matrimony's muddle.

There are other effects of the breakup of so many American homes, however. Recently the media has decried the "feminization of poverty," but much of that poverty is caused by the loss of an intact family's income. The number of female-headed households with one or more children under eighteen doubled from 1970 to 1982, from 2.9 million to 5.9 million, and many of those women now are desperately tired of trying to work, pay for child care, keep their homes, and raise their children all at the same time. Susan Crain Bakos pictures it vividly:

> Carolyn, a retail sales clerk in Lawrence, Kansas, said, "There are days when I would marry the first man with a decent income, the first guy who asked. I didn't get divorced so I could be alone; I got divorced because I had grand illusions about what marriage should be. I was a romantic; and my marriage wasn't romantic. So I left."
>
> When Carolyn left four years ago, at age 30, she regarded poverty as something of a grand adventure. "I knew it would be tight at first, but I told myself it would get better. . . . Well, I forgot one thing: Paul had a future when I married him. I didn't have a future when I married me. . . . I never meant to end up this way."[8]

Along with the breakup of our homes, we are suffering from the effects of sexual permissiveness. When our now-grown daughter entered college, her major problem was not adjusting to a new life away from home; it was dealing with a roommate who insisted on having her boyfriend sleep with her in the room on weekends. "That's just something you have to get used to in college," a dorm mate told our daughter. "Don't worry about it," counseled the university chaplain. Our daughter did worry about it and quickly found herself another roommate, while the college solved the problem for everyone by housing all "sexually active" women in one wing of the dorm. It was typical of the modern college scene. Seventy-five percent of all women now have intercourse before marriage, a rise from 47 percent in 1960–65, and this has spawned an epidemic of genital herpes, which is incurable even with our present wonder drugs. The disease can lead to infant death, unless a child is delivered by cesarian section to prevent infection by the mother.

Worst of all, such sexual permissiveness has resulted in an epidemic of teenage pregnancy. Over 20 percent of all white children born in the United States are illegitimate, over 60 percent of all black children, and the largest proportion are born to teenage mothers. But the children of such child mothers face a dismal future.

> As infants, they have high rates of illness and mortality. Later in life, they often experience educational and emotional problems. Many are victims of child abuse at the hands of parents too immature to understand why their baby is crying or how their doll-like plaything has suddenly developed a will of its own. Finally, these children of children are prone to dropping out and becoming teenage parents themselves.... "A lot of the so-called feminization of poverty starts off with teenagers having babies," said a state expert in Atlanta. "So many can't rise above it to go back to school or get job skills."[9]

Social workers are almost unanimous in citing the influence of the popular media—television, rock music, videos, movies—in propelling youngsters toward precocious sexuality. But our whole culture has fostered the belief that permissive sexual practices are acceptable and without cost, and now we are paying the price of that folly—in lives ruined, futures cut off, children stunted and abused, not to mention the $8.6 billion that the United States spends each year on income support for teenagers who are pregnant or have given birth.

We are also paying the price of the promiscuous and aberrant sexual practices that have contributed to the rapid spread of AIDS in this country. Up to the middle of 1986, 22,000 cases of AIDS had been reported in the United States, over half of them already ended in death, and it is projected by federal officials that in the next ten years there will be 270,000 cases, with 179,000 deaths. The monetary medical cost of that alone will be $8 billion to $16 billion. Nor will the disease be limited to homosexuals and intravenous drug users. It will be spread by heterosexual relations to 7,000 people by 1991, and to 3,000 children.

Finally, our sexual "freedom," which in reality has enslaved us to horrible consequences, has resulted in an epidemic of abortion. One out of every four pregnancies in the United States is now terminated by abortion—a mind-boggling slaughter of new life. While abortion is sometimes justified (in cases of rape and incest, for example), it does something to the moral fiber of a nation when abortion is used as a means of birth control in relation to promiscuous sexuality or as a tool of convenience in life-style planning.

These are the facts of American life and sociology that the preacher confronts when he or she stands up in the pulpit to speak of family concerns, and every preacher needs to be very conscious of them, because they form the climate in which our people live and they influence our people's thought and behavior in the most fundamental ways. That the pulpit should be silent over against such cultural practices is inconceivable. That it should acquiesce to them would be sinful.

To these basic sociological facts of American home life should be added those in two other categories, however, and of them too the preacher should be aware.

First, no homiletician can deal adequately with family concerns these days without taking into account the women's movement. In the last twenty-five years, the struggle for equal rights for women has drastically altered society's views of the proper roles for both females and males. It used to be that we knew automatically the places that husbands and wives should assume in our society. The man went out to work; the woman stayed home and cared for the house and children, finding her fulfillment and satisfaction in her role as homemaker and, vicariously, through her husband's status and achievement. Now women have discovered that they have skills and talents of their own, and they have begun to make very positive contributions in their own right. Fully 60 percent of them are now in the labor market. At the same time, many husbands and fathers have assumed a much larger share of responsibility for child rearing, although women still are usually expected to keep the house and take primary care of the children, even when working full-time outside of the home.

The point is that expectations have changed. Roles are no longer clearly defined, and new expectations for the marital relationship have been introduced. Women now seek full sharing and equality and companionship with their husbands. This has been a marvelous achievement and certainly one that should be encouraged. But it has also had the effect of putting new strains on marital and home relationships. Marriage has become much more of an experimental relationship than it ever was before. More is now expected of the union, but at the same time there are no guidelines to go by. Each couple is on its own, left to adjust the respective roles of husband and wife according to their individual circumstances.

With so many women working outside the home, schedules have had to be adjusted, child care provided, circumstances of promotions and career changes arbitrated between spouses. Many women are postponing childbirth until their 30s, with concomitant medical risks. Others are trying to work full-time while meeting the demands of motherhood and home-making—a double duty which, they have found, leaves them totally exhausted and feeling guilty that perhaps they are neglecting their children. More and more women and men are not marrying at all, choosing to give priority to career rather than to home life, and single people now account for 23 percent of all U.S. households. Those who do marry are doing so later in life, with the median age now 25.4 years for men and 23 years for women.

Second, the number of older persons in our population is growing rapidly. One out of four Americans is now over the age of 50, and on the whole they are doing well. Most of them are healthy, vigorous, and solvent. They control three quarters of the nation's financial assets and possess $130 billion in discretionary income. In 1965, one third of the over-65 group were classified below the poverty line; today only 14 percent are. By the year 2025, there will be 64 million people over the age of 65; by just the year 2000, the number over 85 will double. There will be fewer than four working persons for every retirement-age individual, a ratio that will put a severe strain on the already overburdened Social Security system. Our health programs have paid off by giving us longer and more independent lives, but the aging of the population will increasingly bring problems of support for the elderly, of their health care and housing and employment. Already, in every congregation, some members face the dilemma of how responsibly to care for elderly parents and of how to include them in home life. This will increasingly become a problem for the church and its individual members.

Change! That fact now characterizes the American home. There is no church congregation, no matter how conservative, that is not affected by change. But where you have change, you get experimentation; and where you get experimentation, you have some failures. Preachers must minister to their people in the

midst of almost dizzying change, bringing the light of
the gospel to bear on every new or changing circum-
stance. That such a ministry requires the most thor-
ough knowledge of the gospel and the most sensitive
awareness of our people's and society's ways, plus the
ability to reflect on the relation of the one to the other,
cannot be overemphasized.

3

Dealing with Basic
Presuppositions

It is obvious that a book of this size—or of any size, for that matter—cannot deal with every area of family life, nor can a preacher treat all those areas from the pulpit. To deal thoroughly with family concerns would involve not only all the issues we have raised thus far but also matters of employment, housing, money, leisure, health, entertainment, conflict, child rearing, and on and on—indeed, all of the matters connected with human birth, life, and death, for it is as a member of a family that most of our life is lived out. Human beings are familial creatures; family constitutes, surrounds, and to a large measure creates who we are and what we become. When the Christian church baptizes us into the family of God the Father, it is dealing with one of the most determinative contexts of our lives.

The preacher therefore needs to address the basics of family concerns, lest the primary presuppositions of Christian family life get lost in a multitude of details. To be sure, many of the detailed matters can and should be touched on in other sermons, used as illustrative materials, referred to from time to time. But the gospel for families is so important that its basic presuppositions should be spelled out first of all, and in this chapter we want to consider some of those foundational positions. The discussion will be continued in the following chapters, as we spell out the

biblical view of marriage and family. Right now, let us
begin to consider some of the presuppositions that
grow out of that biblical view.

First of all, it is basic to the Christian faith that it is
primarily concerned with human relationships. There
is no way, according to the Bible, that one can be a
Christian all by oneself. As soon as one enters into
fellowship with the God and Father of our Lord Jesus
Christ, one is set under the command to love others.
"By this all men will know that you are my disciples,
if you have love for one another" (John 13:35). "For
the whole law is fulfilled in one word, 'You shall love
your neighbor as yourself' " (Gal. 5:14). "So if you are
offering your gift at the altar, and there remember that
your brother has something against you, leave your
gift there before the altar and go; first be reconciled
to your brother, and then come and offer your gift"
(Matt. 5:23–24). "Truly, I say to you, as you did it to
one of the least of these my brethren, you did it to me"
(Matt. 25:40). The relationship with God is never separated in the scriptures from the relationship with
one's fellows. And so the mystical union with God, the
ascetic retreat from the world, the beatific vision, the
relation of the individual to his or her Lord, the acceptance of the individual into heaven—these finally
are not the goal of the Christian faith. Rather, the
whole of the Bible testifies that God seeks, above all
else, a new community, in which persons live together
in love and peace and righteousness under his guiding
lordship. Every power of the Word and Spirit is di-
rected, in the Bible's story, toward the creation of that
community, toward the time when God's kingdom will
have come on earth, even as it is in heaven.

In short, the God of the Bible deals with us not only
as individuals but also as community members—in the
community of marriage, as married couples, and as
parents and as children. And the saving influence of
God's Holy Spirit effects changes not only within individuals but also within relationships among wives

and husbands and children. God has transformed us in Jesus Christ, not only as single persons but also as married couples, and for a husband or wife to ignore that corporate working of the Lord is to ignore the goal of the gospel. Thus, for a husband to say, "I love God, but I cannot love my wife," is a contradiction in terms (see 1 John 4:20–21). Or the supposedly "religious" wife who looks down in scorn on her "irreligious" husband has not understood the Christian faith. In the biblical faith, every family relationship affects the relationship with God, just as, vice versa, God is at work in every area and relationship of family life.

Second, it is characteristic of the people of God throughout the Bible that they are to live lives uniquely different from that style of living found in the society around them. In the Old Testament, the people of Israel are a people set apart for God's purpose; they are God's "holy nation" (Ex. 19:6; see also 1 Peter 2:9). Thus the oracles of Balaam can describe Israel as "a people dwelling alone, and not reckoning itself among the nations" (Num. 23:9), and the law of Moses commands the Israelites to live by God's commandments and not by the customs and laws of their environment:

> I am the LORD your God. You shall not do as they do in the land of Egypt, where you dwelt, and you shall not do as they do in the land of Canaan, to which I am bringing you. You shall not walk in their statutes. You shall do my ordinances and keep my statutes and walk in them. I am the LORD your God. You shall therefore keep my statutes and my ordinances, by doing which a man shall live: I am the LORD. (Leviticus 18:2–5)

In the New Testament, in like fashion, Christians are not to be conformed to this world but are to be transformed by the renewal of their minds, after the mind of Christ, so that they do the will of God and walk by his Spirit and not according to the spirit of their age (Rom. 12:1; Phil. 2:5; Rom. 8:11–14; Eph. 4:11–16). Indeed, so different is the Christian life from the life of the world that others can note a radical change in manner of living among new converts to the faith (1 Peter 4:3–4).

Faith in the God of the Bible sets one under a new requirement—the requirement to live according to God's will and ways, given us in the scriptures, rather than according to the will and ways of the world. "If you love me, you will keep my commandments," Jesus says (John 14:15). And faith in the God of Jesus Christ brings with it that powerful and transforming Spirit who enables one so to live (John 14:16–17; Gal. 2:20).

Applied to marriage and home, then, this means that Christian marriages and home life are uniquely different from those in the society around them. George Will once wrote a column in *Newsweek* in which he recalled a statement of Charles Peguy's that "the true revolutionaries in our society are the parents of Christian families."[1] How true that is! Christian families are now so different from the usual families in our society that they are revolutionary.

For example, in the Christian marriage ceremony, partners vow to honor and love one another as long as they both shall live, but that has been diluted in our culture until it has come to mean "as long as they both shall love." "We have been misled with overly inflated expectations about marriage," wrote a professor of philosophy at the State University of New York at Binghamton. "You can't say you'll love someone forever because it's just not a promise you can realistically make. What we should be saying is, 'I love you now and I hope I'll love you a year from now; I'll work at it.' A better marriage vow may be one designed to protect the offspring of that marriage, one that spells out financial obligations in case of divorce."[2] Thus, our society has lost all hope in relationship to marriage, and persons now have come to view it as such a risky and transient relationship that their only thought is to protect themselves and their offspring financially when the inevitable divorce occurs. To believe Christian marriage is possible, to believe that it can be a lifelong and faithfully joyful union of two people loving one another, establishing their home, doing their work, raising their family, and growing closer and closer together over the years—yes, that is revolutionary in our day and our society.

But Christians were made to be revolutionaries. We were called by God into his church to live the new life of the new age of the kingdom of God in this world. That kingdom has broken into our world in the person of Jesus Christ (Mark 1:15; Luke 11:20), bringing with it all the power of God to forgive and reconcile, to heal and transform, to guide and sustain. And it is now by the power of that kingdom, granted us through faith in Christ, that we are to walk our daily ways and live out our family lives. As George Will further put it, "Christianity is a religion of unadjusted people whose obligation is to adjust to something that transcends the culture of the day, any day."[3] We are called to adjust our lives to the lordship of God in Jesus Christ, and that has always been revolutionary.

Third, in dealing with the basic presuppositions of biblical faith in relation to our homes, the preacher needs to examine very carefully from the pulpit our views with regard to God's commandments that have been given us in the scriptures. Christians are those who join the New Testament church in its earliest confession that "Jesus is Lord" (see 1 Cor. 12:3; 16:22), and that confession implies that we are therefore subject to the commands of that Lord. But so distorted has the understanding of Christian doctrine become in our time, and so relativistic has become the approach to the scriptures, that many persons in the church are now convinced they stand under no commands at all. A Methodist seminary professor once stated to me that Jesus issued no commandments! Other persons hold that the doctrine of justification by faith excludes all necessity of obedience. And some Christians are so ignorant of the scriptures or have so abandoned the scriptures' authority that their knowledge of the nature of God has become completely distorted. They believe God only forgives, that he lays no requirements upon us, and that therefore any way of life is acceptable and permissible in the Christian church. God will accept anybody, goes the predominant view; we may just go on sinning in order that his forgiving grace toward us may abound (cf. Rom. 6:1).

The whole New Testament, and indeed the Old, contradicts such views. It is the one who hears Jesus' words and does them who is like a wise man who built his house upon the rock (Matt. 7:24–27). It is the one who takes up Jesus' guiding yoke and learns from him who finds rest for her soul (Matt. 11:29). The church is to teach all nations to observe all that Jesus has commanded (Matt. 28:20). And those who say to him simply, "Lord, Lord," will not enter the kingdom, but rather those who do the will of his Father who is in heaven (Matt. 7:21). Thus, Paul can list the deeds of human beings that will exclude them from the kingdom of God (1 Cor. 6:9–10; Gal. 5:19–21), and Jesus can say to those who have neglected mercy, "Depart from me, you cursed" (Matt. 25:41).

Is this legalism? Does the necessity of obedience to the commands of our Lord contradict the basic Protestant understanding of justification by faith alone? And does it therefore finally mean that none of us is or will be acceptable to our God? Surely, if that were the case, it would be reason for hopelessness and despair!

The commandments of God, given us in the scriptures, have three functions. First, they convict us of our sin. They show us vividly how far we have fallen short of God's intention for our lives. Second, they bring home to us the necessity of the Gospel—the fact that we are indeed lost unless we can cast ourselves wholly on the forgiveness and mercy of God for the sole source of our salvation into eternal life and escape from the death that our sinful ways merit.

But the commandments of our Lord, given us in the Bible, have a third function: They serve as a guide to how we are to live in the new life that we have in fact been given through the mercy and forgiveness of Jesus Christ. Sincere Christians therefore obey the commands and directions of their Lord, not *in order that* they may be made acceptable to God but *because* they have already been accepted through the death and resurrection of Jesus Christ. In short, we respond in gratitude and obedience to this One who has redeemed and justified us. We respond in heartfelt morality to the Son of God, who, because of his sacrifice, has been given that name that is above every name (Phil. 2:5–11).

This response, moreover, is not a matter of legalism but one of the deepest trust. Why do children willingly obey a parent? Certainly not out of fear of punishment or fear of the consequences of some action, but because they trust that the parent loves them and has their good at heart. Children trust their parents to show them the right way and to give them good things.

So it is too in our relationship with God. We obey God's commandments for us, because finally we trust him. We trust that he has nothing but our good at heart. We trust that he loves us and wants abundant life for us. We trust that no matter what happens to us, God means us good and is working toward that good in our lives (Rom. 8:28).

Therefore, when we read the commandments of God in the scriptures that have to do with marriage and sex, with home and children, with divorce and the elderly, we trust that God has given us such commandments because he loves us and wants us to have abundant life. As Deuteronomy so cogently puts it, these commandments are "for our good always," that we may have life (6:24; see also 10:13). How true that

seems to be when we look at the wreckage in our
faithless society's homes and families! Could it be, for
example, that when God forbid fornication, he knew
the consequences of such disobedient evil? To trust
God means to believe that he alone knows the way to
abundant life, and to act accordingly.

Fourth, in dealing with the Bible's basic presuppositions about home and family, the preacher should illumine for the congregation the nature of commitment,
because that finally is the bedrock upon which every
Christian home is built—commitment to God through
Jesus Christ and commitment to one's family.

The scriptures condemn two types of phony commitment. First is that which results in insincerity: actions taken apart from the involvement of the heart.
Thus, throughout the prophetic writings, the people
of Israel are castigated for worship and service of God
that does not involve their hearts (see Isa. 29:13–14;
Jer. 4:1–4), just as they are similarly condemned for
deceitful actions toward their fellows (Jer. 9:2–9). In
like manner, Paul shows to be worthless all religious
acts that do not involve the heart (1 Cor. 13). Surely
such insincerity is found in our time in every one of
those church weddings in which a couple takes vows
"before God and this company" with no intention or
knowledge of trusting commitment to God!

The scriptures also condemn that phony commitment which vows loyalty apart from action—that son
who says he will go and work in the vineyard but does
not do so (Matt. 21:28–32), those disciples who vow
loyalty unto death but desert their Master when the
crunch comes (Mark 14:26–31), those followers who
zealously promise faithfulness but want to act it out
sometime in the future (Luke 9:57–62). They are like
so many of us Christians who vow so often to be faithful to God in our home life but can find a dozen ration-
alizations and excuses for making exceptions to the
vow: It seemed "the loving thing to do," or "the best
course of action," or "better for the children," or "the

only way I could find myself," or "better for all concerned." As with Eve in the garden, our sin always
looks like the "right thing to do" at the time (see Gen.
3:6); the difficulty is that it directly contradicts the
commandment of God (Gen. 2:16–17).

Reinhold Niebuhr once made the profound statement that "love involves the willingness to take responsibility." No thought is more true of Christian
home life; it always involves the willingness to take
responsibility—in short, to act out inner loyalty and
love. A lot of young couples have convinced themselves these days that marriage licenses are unnecessary, that they are in fact committed to one another,
and that matrimony is an unnecessary addition to their
heartfelt love. Thus, the number of unmarried couples
living together has been growing by an average of
107,000 per year since 1970, and as of March 1984,
there were 1,983,000 unmarried-couple households,
according to the Census Bureau. But the truth is that
marriage licenses are more than pieces of paper; they
are evidence of the willingness to take responsibility.

Because I am legally married to my husband and
have a state marriage license, I also am legally responsible when the joint income tax form comes up for an
audit, or when he is involved in a traffic accident, or
for his actions in our neighborhood, just as he is legally responsible with me for the children born of our
union. Marriage licenses say, "I will take responsibility
for this other person—legal, public, hard-fact responsibility"—and unless two people are willing to accept
such full responsibility for their union, they have not
truly committed themselves to one another. Thus, it is
precisely this unwillingness to be responsible for the
actions of the other that characterizes the sinful relation of Adam and Eve in that profound story of Genesis 3 (vs. 12–13).

Love and commitment involve responsibility and
care for another besides oneself, and love, according
to the scriptures, never remains simply an inner emo-

tion but always manifests itself in concrete outward action. God loves his people Israel (Hos. 11:1; see also Deut. 7:7), and that involves his deepest inner yearning for their fellowship and answering love (Jer. 3:19). But the love of God never remains simply an inner emotion. Rather, it is acted out in God's delivery of Israel from slavery in Egypt, in his guidance of his wandering people through the terrors of the wilderness and his daily sustenance of them, in his gift to them of the promised land and of the promised Davidic kingship. Finally and fully, God's love is acted out in his gift of his only Son that not only Israel but all persons might have eternal life. Love is a verb in the Bible; it never remains just a noun. And because we Christians are to be "imitators of God, as beloved children," we too are to act out our love and our commitment to one another in our homes, walking "in love, as Christ loved us and gave himself up for us" (Eph. 5:1–2).

Such an understanding of love and commitment gives the lie to the spirit of our time—to that selfish quest for personal fulfillment and happiness, regardless of others, so typical of our culture. For example, some years ago Caroline Bird, who wrote the book *Born Female,* gave a lecture on marriage to some students at Westhampton College in Virginia. This is what the newspaper reported about it:

> Miss Bird suggested that the increasing longevity and choices about lifestyles will mean that people will marry two or three different people in their lifetime, each for different reasons. "Divorces will be quite friendly," she said. "People will outgrow people."
> . . . The successive relationships that Miss Bird envisions will help each partner fill certain developmental needs. [There we have the emphasis solely on one's own needs.] "Your first love is usually a defense against your parents, someone to help you get away from home. But he or she may be a very inappropriate

partner for your next task." Career development, iden-
tity search and children are other reasons Miss Bird
mentioned for getting married. "You need to formal-
ize the commitment as parents," she said, "but the
commitment doesn't need to outlast the child-raising
years. Generally speaking, people who have a series of
serious love affairs grow up better." And besides, she
added, "Women are increasingly getting what they
need for the next step in their development from their
women friends."[4]

In short, in this view, which typifies the views of so
many in our society, marriages and homes are used to
get what you need, to satisfy your own selfish and
ingrown desires. My first reaction is that this attitude
may well be appropriate for a one-month-old infant,
but it certainly is not to be expected from a supposedly
grown-up woman. But it is characteristic of many persons in our culture, and when one reads such statements, it becomes very clear why so many of our
homes are falling apart.

Over against such views, our Lord promises us that
"whoever would save his life will lose it; and whoever
loses his life for my sake and the gospel's will save it"
(Mark 8:35 and pars.). Christians are called, in their
homes, to the most strenuous love and service for
others. And in assessing the claims of that call, perhaps we should ask ourselves, Which claims better
honor the human personality, those set forth by persons like Caroline Bird or by Christians like Paul of
Tarsus? What do we want—to use and manipulate
other people, just to get what we desire? Or do we
want to use all our capacities to grow up into the
measure of the fullness of the stature of Christ, into
mature manhood and womanhood? Listen to Paul:

Love is patient and kind; love is not jealous or boastful;
it is not arrogant or rude. Love does not insist on its
own way; it is not irritable or resentful; it does not
rejoice at wrong, but rejoices in the right. Love bears

all things, believes all things, hopes all things, endures
all things. Love never ends. (1 Corinthians 13:4–8)

Is that not the picture of what we are supposed to be?
Does it not honor us, dignify us, call us to our highest
purpose, and make all the struggles we go through
worthwhile for the purpose? The human personality
has more worth than our "me generation" would give
it. And we are called not to the twisting, rocky road of
selfishness, which tramps through a swamp of sin and
ends up going nowhere. We are called to the high
morning road of faith, which leads to goodness in the
human personality, and the light, and the love of Jesus
Christ.

As is the case with all God's directions for our lives,
the call for such love and commitment in our home life
is once again a manifestation of God's desire that we
have abundant life, for apart from such total commitment of ourselves to the way of Christ and to each
other, Christian family life is impossible.

No marriage is likely long to survive unless there is
total commitment on the part of the spouses. To be
sure, marriages may be held together by other considerations: by economic necessity, by concern for the
children, by social pressure or legalistic strictures, or
even by habit, but such marriages are not very likely
to have about them the characteristic of "abundant
life." That life comes from unstinting commitment to
the relationship—commitment that says, "Come what
may, we will remain together in love. Though you
become blind tomorrow, I will be there. Though you
be a 'success' or a 'failure,' I will be there. Though we
suffer, fight, struggle, work hard, lose dreams, or fulfill
them, we will go through it all together, and as Christ
has never deserted us, so we will never desert one
another."

Strangely enough, it is that commitment to the
other which then gives the Christian the freedom
within marriage fully to develop that personhood our

selfish society so covets. For if a couple knows they will stay together, no matter what; if divorce is unthinkable for them, and they are absolutely committed to staying together, then they know that every fight does not threaten the marriage, and so they can be absolutely open and honest with one another. They can communicate their real feelings, work out their actual problems, develop their true selves, without the fear that each disagreement will break apart the relationship. As Jerry M. Lewis, psychiatrist-in-chief at Timberlawn Hospital in Dallas has pointed out, couples in healthy marriages "have a deep level of intimate communication which they described to researchers as 'the most remarkable thing that ever happened in my life' because of the openness and freedom to talk about deep feelings and thoughts."[5]

It is commitment that gives that freedom in marriage—as it is always commitment that gives freedom (see John 8:31–32; 2 Cor. 3:17)—and it is only in that commitment that freedom is to be found. If we start out with reservations in marriage, to see if we can get along, or if we are just living together to try it out, we do not have that freedom that comes from absolute commitment. And so we cannot fight and disagree and open up our hearts to one another, for fear that the other will disapprove and leave. "Whoever would save his life will lose it"—whoever would seek only his or her own welfare in marriage will lose the abundant life that a lasting and faithful marriage can bring with it— "but whoever loses his life will save it"—whoever gives himself or herself totally to the marital relationship will find joyful life and personhood given back to them. Our Lord made that promise to us because he loves us.

4

What Does the Bible Say?

A preacher has no other authority than that lent to him or her by the biblical Word, for it is through the Bible's history that God reveals himself to us, and it is through the Bible's Word that God acts among his gathered people to judge and to save, to "pluck up and to pull down . . . to build and to plant." Insofar as a sermon is built upon the biblical Word, it may share in God's power—when God sees fit—to work his will among his people. Otherwise the sermon is just one more address, setting forth the ideas and opinions of just one more person.

The first question that any preacher has to ask in relation to any family concern, therefore, is, What does the Bible say? But the preacher asks that question not to find proof texts, not to uncover legalistic principles for the congregation's life, not to read the Bible as a static Word spoken once and for all, but rather to hear the living God speaking by the Holy Spirit through the dynamics of a history that has taken place and that continues to reveal God's will and action in our present and our future.

To hear the Bible's living Word on behalf of his or her congregation, the preacher brings to the biblical text all the careful scholarship and critical study, all the faith, all the prayer in the Spirit of which he or she is capable. And then the preacher listens—listens for

the Word for God's people. And that Word becomes
the content of the sermon. Thus, in relation to family
concerns, What does the Bible say?

About Human Nature

On its first two pages, the Bible presents us with a
marvelous and unique view of human nature: We are
created, it confesses, male and female, in the image of
God (Gen. 1:26–27). This is the basic definition of our
humanity—that we can be understood only in relation
to God. And this means that in any discussion of family
concerns the Christian faith is not simply one more
topic to be considered alongside all the rest. So often
in books about marriage there will be chapters dealing
with various matters important for a happy home:
communication, money, sexual relations, fighting
fairly, and so forth. And then finally there will be one
chapter on religious faith—as if that were just one
more element necessary to add to the list. But because
we cannot be understood apart from our relation to
God, the Christian faith forms the context of all other
aspects of home life. None of the other topics having
to do with family concerns can properly be understood apart from the relation to God, because human
beings cannot be understood apart from that relationship.

Our culture continually tries to define us in other,
lesser terms, of course. A leading news magazine
defined us some time ago as "essentially animals." To
economists, we may be nothing more than producers
or consumers; to government, taxpayers or statistics.
The medical profession may view us as collections of
cells and genes; psychologists, as ids, drives, and
needs. The Pentagon may glibly define us in the grisly
terms of body counts, and the politicians may see us
as nothing more than votes in a key precinct. Or let us
put it in positive terms: The humanist may even say
that the human personality is a marvel and a mystery,

possessed with potentialities for love and creativity beyond all calculation, shaping history by the use of language and enriching life with the arts, free to mold the stuff of the universe to accord with the highest dreams and aspirations. And to that exalted definition of our nature, the Bible replies: This is not enough, because the human person can fully be defined only in relation to God. Precisely that fact ultimately protects our humanity and shields us from the manipulation and misuse of our persons by any group or ideology. When our relationship to God is omitted, our society goes awry, and we have to have some sort of revolution to reclaim our personhood (such as, in our time, the feminist movement). We are made in the image of God: That is the basic beginning statement of the Bible concerning human beings.

We are given the image of God, according to Genesis, in order that we may have dominion over the earth (1:26–30). We are to rule over and tend and keep God's created world. But our dominion is a secondary rule. Just as an emperor in ancient times set up statues of himself throughout his empire to show his rule over it, so God the King erects us, his statues, his little images on the face of the earth, that we may point to his rule over every corner of his creation. (Thus, when we journey into distant space, we are taking the *imago dei* with us and proclaiming not *our* rule over the moon and the universe but God's sovereignty over them.) That, affirm the priestly writers of Genesis, is the purpose of human life—finally to point to God's lordship over all his creation. In the words of the Shorter Catechism, the chief purpose of our lives is "to glorify God, and to enjoy him forever." Or, in the words of Jesus, "Let your light so shine before men, that they may see your good works and give glory to your Father who is in heaven" (Matt. 5:16). That is God's intention for human life. That is why we are here.

Clearly, the Christian doctrine of the creation of human beings in the image of God possesses a wonderful balance. On the one hand, it affirms that we are glorious creatures, unlike any other in all creation, made for relation with our Maker. And this teaching wars against every attempt to degrade the human personality or to subject it to any absolute rule besides that of the Creator. But the doctrine also affirms that we are in fact creatures, subject to the sovereignty of our Creator, and therefore no one of us can claim absolute rights. We have no right to make our own experience the absolute measure of good (as many feminist theologians are doing, for example), any more than we have the prerogative to claim absolute right over our own bodies (as one hears the pro-choice advocates saying). No. "The LORD is God. It is he that made us, and not we ourselves. We are his people, and the sheep of his pasture" (Ps. 100:3). Finally, we belong to God and are subject to his rule and his shepherding of us.

It is also important in our particular culture to note that, in Genesis 1, sexuality is a part of creation and therefore not attributable to God the Creator. In the biblical faith, God is always understood as totally Other—that is, as "holy," unique, completely different from his created world. Therefore all contemporary arguments over the sexuality of God have misunderstood the biblical witness, and to understand God the Father as a "male God" is totally to misunderstand his nature.

Further, because sexuality is a structure of creation and not of the Creator, human sexual relations are never understood in the scriptures to participate in the divine realm or to reveal it. We do not participate in "something divine" in the ecstasy of intercourse. The feminist Starhawk has maintained that "in orgasm, we share in the force that moves the stars,"[1] but that was the view of the Baal religion that surrounded Israel, and the prophets fought against it with every means at their disposal.

By the same token, because sexuality is a structure

of creation, the marital relation is a part of this world only, and like all of this world in the biblical view, it is not eternal but transitory. The institution of marriage passes away with this world. There is no marrying or giving in marriage in the kingdom of God, Jesus tells us (Mark 12:18–25 and pars.), and therefore the marriage bond obtains only "until death does us part." Marriage, therefore, cannot be viewed as the be-all and end-all of existence, and the final purpose of our living is not to get married and live happily ever after but to serve the Creator and Lord who has made and redeemed us. Single persons are fully as able to realize God's purpose for their lives as are married persons—both Jesus and the apostle Paul were unmarried, and Jesus is quite specific about the fact that there are some who are called to remain single for the sake of the kingdom of God (Matt. 19:10–12).

All these statements grow out of the careful theological witness of Genesis 1, formulated for us across centuries of theological reflection and of experience of the Lord of Israel. As we have seen, they form the biblical corrective for many of the aberrant views propounded by some in our society.

About Marriage

The interesting phenomenon in the Bible is that when it wants to spell out in detail the foundations of marriage and the home, it does so not in the form of theological statements but in the form of a story. It tells us about a man and a woman in a garden, because stories have the character of letting us enter into them and identify with them. Indeed, the Bible wishes us to understand the stories of Genesis 2–11 as our story, for "Adam" is the Hebrew word for "humankind." This is the story of our lives, the way we all have walked in relation to God. And in this story we find the foundational understanding of the Christian home.

The intention of God for Christian marriage is set

forth very clearly in Genesis 2. God is pictured in thought, and we have that wonderful portrayal of the Lord musing to himself. "It is not good that the man should be alone," he says (v. 18). I have often thought that to be one of the most merciful passages in the Bible, for right there at the beginning of the story, we hear that we were not meant to be alone—not meant to be isolated, self-fulfilling egos, turned in on ourselves, concerned only with our own well-being, and growing more and more selfish about our own comforts and needs as we age. No, we were created to have relationships with other human beings. Intimacy with the natural world does not satisfy Adam in the story (vs. 19–20). He needs someone with whom he can share his life, in love and care and mutual helpfulness. And that, in fact, is the meaning of the Hebrew phrase, "I will make a helper fit for him" (v. 18). "Fit for him" has the meaning of "corresponding to him." God sets out to make a partner for the man who will complement his life—one in whom he sees himself and with whom he can share and commune.

Thus there follows in the story the creation of the woman out of the rib of the man (vs. 21–22). The Bible is saying that once the man and his wife were one, so that after her creation they long to become one again. Then we find another marvelous picture: God, the Father of the bride, brings the woman to the man, and the man cries out, in ecstatic joy, "This at last is bone of my bones and flesh of my flesh" (v. 23); that is, "Here at last is the one in whom I see myself, with whom I can join my life in fellowship." The man and the woman therefore become one flesh, in the joyful new community of marriage.

Here, in the strongest terms, the Bible is affirming the marital relation. Husband and wife are both naked, but they are not ashamed (v. 25). The body, the desire of the sexes for one another, the marital union of corresponding helpfulness, the resulting family— these, the Bible is saying to us, are the merciful gifts of a loving God. And our Lord affirms this goodness of the marital relation in Mark 10:7–9: "They are no longer two but one. What therefore God has joined together, let not man put asunder."

Does this mean, then, that every marriage is "made in heaven" and that God has willed the union of every couple we find in society? Of course not. Some marriages are consummated for the basest of reasons or in the most awful circumstances—sometimes when the participants are roaring drunk—and as with every other gift of God, according to the biblical faith, God's merciful gift of the new community of Christian marriage must be appropriated in faith by the couple. Insofar as by faith God's gift is received, he ordains and prospers the relationship. That is the joyful good news granted to the faithful Christian couple. For if God be for us, who can be against us? Every married couple is invited by the Gospel to make that good news their own, and every marriage can be redeemed by opening the relationship to God's work within it. But that working is received and appropriated only by faith—by trust in and dependence on God and not on ourselves.

The goodness of marriage, as God intends it, is affirmed for us throughout the scriptures. When Jeremiah wants to picture Judah restored after the exile, he does so by portraying the mirth and gladness of a wedding (33:10–11), just as Third Isaiah describes the delight of that restoration in terms of marriage (62:4–5). The marital relation is a source of joy, something to celebrate, and so the Psalms exult over the blessings of marriage and children (Pss. 127:3–5; 128:3–6), and both Proverbs (5:18) and Ecclesiastes (9:9) urge upon husbands enjoyment of life with the wife whom they love. It is with his wife that Isaac is comforted at his mother's death (Gen. 24:67), and the prophet Malachi describes "the wife of your youth" as your "companion," while Proverbs 18:22 maintains that "he who finds a wife finds a good thing, and obtains favor from the LORD." Obviously the marital relation is understood as one of satisfaction and joy.

In fact, so good is the gift of marriage that, throughout the scriptures, the marital relation is made a metaphor of God's relation with his people. Not only in Hosea (chs. 1–3), but also in Isaiah and Jeremiah and Ezekiel, Israel is frequently spoken of as God's wife (Isa. 50:1; 54:4–6) or bride (Isa. 62:5; Jer. 2:2), and the Lord is the Husband who has entered into a marriage covenant with his people (Jer. 3:20; Ezek. 16; Isa. 62:4). In the New Testament, Jesus is compared to the figure of the bridegroom (Mark 2:19–20 and pars.; John 3:29), and Paul states that through faith the church is presented as a pure bride to Christ (2 Cor. 11:2). In Ephesians, the union of husband and wife is the concrete symbol of Christ's union with his church (5:31–32). In Revelation, when the coming kingdom of God is portrayed, it is pictured as a marriage (Rev. 19:6–9; 21:2, 9–11).

Perhaps it is this understanding of the marital relation that needs to be emphasized from the pulpit— that it is a merciful gift of God, intended to bring with it blessing and joy, companionship and comfort. Marriage has received a bad press in our time—literally, a very bad press. So many marriages have failed and so distorted has the media's depiction of the relationship been, so fearful are our young people of entering into matrimony, and so repressive has marriage been understood to be by some feminists, that surely first of all the preacher needs to set forth the joy intended in marriage by God. Christian marriage should be celebrated by the church, anniversaries marked and acclaimed, in order that over against the evil propaganda of our time, God's good gift may be known. Christian marriage is definitely a possibility, and indeed a reality, in thousands of our homes. Every congregation needs to hear those facts affirmed.

In setting forth the goodness of Christian marriage, however, we also need to make it very clear that God's intention is that the relationship be one of lifelong and exclusive fidelity. Adultery is specifically prohibited by Israel's basic law, the Ten Commandments, which made up the list of those acts absolutely forbidden to the people of God (Ex. 20:14; Deut. 5:18). In the Old Testament, adultery was so serious an offense that it was punishable by death for both involved in it (Deut. 22:22–24; Lev. 20:10). It was impossible, in Old Testament thought, for the adulterer to have communion with God (see Jer. 7:9–10; Ps. 50:16–18), just as for Paul it is impossible for adulterers to inherit the kingdom of God (1 Cor. 6:9; see also 1 Thess. 4:3–8). Nor is the commandment softened in Jesus' teaching. Adultery, for our Lord, is not merely an outward physical act but a corruption of the inner self (Matt. 15:19; see also 5:28), and Jesus judges it an offense worthy to be punished in hell (Matt. 5:27–30). Other passages state that adulterers stand under judgment (Mal. 3:5; Heb. 13:4) and bring God's curse on the whole land (Jer. 23:10), causing those who have traffic with them to forfeit their very lives.

There is no biblical passage in which adultery is excused or overlooked because of mitigating circumstances, and our sinful culture, in its easy acceptance of the practice, has opened itself to the wrath of God. Whether the effects of that wrath are seen in the immediate and tragic breakup of so many of our homes— breakups that are threatening the very stability of our nation—or whether its effects are understood as postponed until God's final reckoning with us, we can be very sure, as Paul has put it, that "God is not mocked, for whatever a man sows, that he will also reap" (Gal. 6:7).

About Sex

Because sexual relations are understood in the biblical faith to be gifts given only to the marital union, fornication or premarital or extramarital sexual relations are also condemned by the scriptures (Matt. 15: 19; Mark 7:21; Gal. 5:19; Eph. 5:3, 5), as are seduction, rape, sodomy, bestiality, incest, prostitution, and homosexuality (Lev. 18; 19:20–22, 29; 20:10–21; Rom. 1:26–27; 1 Cor. 6:9). We have heard a great deal in our time about the sexual abuse of children and about incestuous relations forced by fathers upon their daughters—one has only to read the columns of "Dear Abby" to become aware of such corruption. We have mounted national campaigns to halt such abuses. But we have taken much more indifferent attitudes toward other forms of fornication and extramarital sexual relations, replacing the biblical understandings with "situation ethics" and every other form of rationalization promulgated by our faithless culture. The result has been the deadly epidemics and teenage pregnancies that we discussed in chapter 2. When responsibility to God's commandments is lost, human beings suffer the consequences. We are made to be responsible to our Creator: That is the way the universe is structured, there is no getting around it, and our Creator has revealed to us through the scriptures that he intends sexual relations to be a merciful gift given only to married couples.

Moreover, God has shown nothing but his love for us in confining sexual relations to marriage, for at its most profound depths and ecstatic heights, sexual intercourse is a form of knowing. Husband and wife "know" one another, in their physical union, in a way that cannot be duplicated by any other experience—a fact recognized in the Bible by the use of the Hebrew word "know" for intercourse (Gen. 4:1; 1 Sam. 1:19–20). Spouses give themselves to one another, in the totality of their persons—body, mind, and spirit—and receive back, by giving themselves away, a deeper knowledge of their own selves. Indeed, in sexual relations, husband and wife grow in their knowledge of one another over the years. As every happily married couple knows, fully satisfying sexual relations cannot be achieved in one night, or one week, or even one year. The full knowledge of wife and husband for one another is a growing, lifelong experience. And so a wise and loving God has provided that such an intimate form of knowledge is to be gained over a lifetime of living and loving together.

About Divorce

According to the scriptures, there is no doubt that divorce is not the intention of God, and therefore he would never sanction our society's reference to the breakup of a home as "good," or "the best thing to do," or "the proper course of action." God grieves over our broken human relationships, grieves over the terrible tangles and heartbreaking situations that our faithlessness gets us into (see Gen. 6:6; Luke 19:42–44). "I hate divorce," he says in the Book of Malachi, "and covering one's garment with violence. . . . So take heed to yourselves and do not be faithless" (2:16). God knows all about the "violence" of divorce—the violent injury done to the well-being, the dreams, the securities of all involved. Those in any congregation who have gone through the trauma of divorce can be assured that God hates what the experience has done to them, for he did not intend their marriage to turn out that way.

This statement may seem to be contradicted by the easy provision for divorce in Deuteronomy 24:1–4, but Jesus specifically countermands that provision in Mark 10:1–12 (see also Luke 16:18 and Matt. 19:1–9, where a later exception is inserted to conform to rabbinic teaching). So indissoluble is the marital union, according to our Lord, that he equates divorce and remarriage with the sin of adultery (Mark 10:11–12), and Paul affirms Jesus' teaching in 1 Corinthians 7:10–16. It is a specific command from the Lord, Paul says, "that the wife should not separate from her husband (but if she does, let her remain single or else be reconciled to her husband) and that the husband should not divorce his wife" (vs. 10–11). Only if one is mated to an unbeliever is there any slackening of the commandment in the thought of Paul (vs. 15–16); and even then, divorce is a last resort, since the unbeliever may be converted by the Christian partner (vs. 13–14). Paul is dealing with Christian marriage in a pagan environment, just as is the modern-day preacher.

About Male and Female Roles

There are no set roles for husband and wife specified in the scriptures, but there is a strong emphasis on the equal status of men and women—an emphasis arising out of Israel's faith and contrasting sharply with the practices in the environment around her. As we have seen, both female and male are believed to be created equally in the image of God (Gen. 1:27), and in the marital relation they are expected to exercise a mutual helpfulness (Gen. 2:18). Where this is not the case and women are dominated by males, such subordination is considered to be the result of sin (Gen. 3:16), just as the subsequent practice of polygamy is considered a manifestation of the spread of sin (Gen. 4:19).

We therefore find women assuming a wide variety of roles in the Old Testament. They are prophetesses (Ex. 15:21; 2 Kings 22:14–20), judges (Judg. 4–5), queens (1 Kings 19; 2 Kings 11), and participants in commercial enterprises (Prov. 31:16–18, 24). Some of them are honored as models of wisdom (2 Sam. 14; 20:16–22), which, along with the practice of charity within the community (Prov. 31:20), is a characteristic of the ideal wife (Prov. 31:26). The honor of mothers ranks with that of fathers in Israel's basic Decalogue (Ex. 20:12; Deut. 5:16), and their family rights as wives and mothers are legally protected. (This is the import of Gen. 16:5–6 and Gen. 38.) Where the Old Testament contains stories about cruelty toward women or the degradation of them, such stories are intended as protests against such practices in Israel's pagan environment (Gen. 19:8; Judg. 11; 19:22–30).

It was only in postexilic times, after the Zadokite priests in exile compiled legislation for Israel that would ensure her ritual and societal purity and thus prevent the judgment of God from coming on Israel ever again, that women were given a secondary status in Israelite society. Emphasis on the unique mark of the Jew, circumcision, introduced sexuality into the realm of the cult (Gen. 17), from which women were then excluded during times of menstruation (Lev. 15: 19–31) and childbirth (Lev. 12:2–5). Blood was to be used solely as a means of atonement for sin (Lev. 10:17–18; 16; 17:10–11), and the blood of female excretions and childbirth was thought to render them ritually unclean.

Because of this ritual development, women were increasingly segregated in Israelite worship and society, and they had access to the holy only through their men. A woman's court was added to the temple to separate women from the sanctuary, and their religious vows became less valuable and subject to those of their husbands (Num. 27:1–8; 30:1–5). By the intertestamental period, they were not to be seen in public or speak to strangers, they were to be doubly veiled on the street, and they could not testify at a court trial. They could not even teach the Torah to their children—a far cry from the prophetess Huldah's authoritative interpretation of Deuteronomy to King Josiah (2 Kings 22:14–20)—and they themselves were not to be educated. They had become, by 200 B.C., second-class citizens, excluded from the worship of their God, with status scarcely above that of slaves.

The actions of Jesus of Nazareth therefore brought into Israel's life the liberating power of the kingdom of God, and everywhere throughout the Gospels we find him affirming female equality. He engages even an unclean foreign woman in public conversation

(John 4:27). He ignores all laws of ritual impurity (Mark 5:25–34, 35–43). He commends the woman who neglects her household duties to be taught at his feet (Luke 10:33–42). Women too, he affirms, are "daughters of Abraham"—that is, members of the covenant (Luke 13:10–17)—"children of wisdom" (Luke 7:35–50), and examples for faith (Matt. 15:21–28; Mark 14:3–9; Luke 21:1–2; cf. 15:8–10).

It is not surprising therefore that women belonged to the inner circle of Jesus' disciples and are noted as those who provided for Jesus and his followers out of their own means (Luke 8:1–3). Both Luke and John attest that women were the first apostles—that is, witnesses of the resurrection (Luke 24:1–11; John 20:18)—and women then played a leading role in the New Testament church. Along with men, they were baptized and received the Spirit (Acts 2:17; 5:14; 8:12; 16:15), and some of them suffered imprisonment for their faith (8:3; 9:1–2). It is almost certain that Phoebe, in Romans 16:1, was a minister of the church, and that Junias, in Romans 16:7, was not a man but a woman "of note among the apostles." According to Paul and Acts, females were allowed to preach and to pray in worship (1 Cor. 11:5–6), as well as to prophesy and to teach (Acts 21:8–9). "There is neither Jew nor Greek," Paul wrote, "there is neither slave nor free, there is neither male nor female; for you are all one in Christ Jesus. And if you are Christ's, then you are Abraham's offspring, heirs according to promise" (Gal. 3:28–29). The ancient sinful segregation and subjugation of womankind is overcome by the in-breaking power of the kingdom in Jesus Christ, and females are returned to that place of equality and freedom God intended for them in the beginning.

Certainly there are also to be found in the New Testament contradictory views—principally in the pastoral epistles, in 1 Timothy 2:11–15; 2 Timothy 3:6–9; and Titus 2:1–10 (see also 1 Peter 3:1–6; Col. 3:18). Because these views so contrast with those of the Gospels and of the earliest writer in the New Testament, Paul, the scriptural exegete must ask what has given rise to such contradictory positions. These later epistles—which are almost universally recognized, except by the most conservative scholars, not to be from Paul—themselves furnish us with the answers. The New Testament church, in the last decades of the first and early decades of the second century, faced the necessity of consolidating its doctrine and regularizing its polity, over against Judaizers and gnostic heretics, just as a half century earlier Paul had had to regularize the raucous worship practices of those disrupting the worship services in the Corinthian church (1 Cor. 14:26–40). Unfortunately, some of the women in the various congregations went too far in their newfound freedom, as did some of the men. Some females adopted extravagant or provocative dress (1 Tim. 2:9; 1 Peter 3:3–6). Some spent their time gadding about, gossiping, and prying into others' affairs (1 Tim. 5:13). Some, though teaching, were ignoring the dictates of reverence for God, slandering persons, and even becoming alcoholics (Titus 2:3). Most serious of all, a good many—perhaps because of their previous lack of education in the faith—were falling prey to the heretical teachings of gnosticism (2 Tim. 3:1–9), engaging in licentiousness or equally foolish asceticism (1 Tim. 4:1–5). Gnosticism, which valued only the spiritual and not the material realm, was a fertile seedbed of both.

The solution to these problems, unfortunately, was one of expediency. Relying on the strong pressure of cultural patriarchal norms and reverting to rabbinic teachings (1 Tim. 2:11–15), some New Testament congregations urged women to be at least as modest as the Gentile and Jewish women around them (1 Cor. 14:33–36; 1 Peter 3:1–6), to submit to the authority and teaching of their husbands, and to remain silent in the church. This was by no means true in all the early New Testament congregations: Each of the letters of the New Testament arises out of a particular church or region, and, as we have seen, both Romans 16 and Acts show that many women continued in leadership positions in the early churches. The unfortunate fact is that, in our day, some biblical interpreters have removed portions of the writings of the New Testament from their historical contexts and applied them, without further ado, to our modern situation as universal rules to be obeyed. But no biblical interpreter can justly ignore the freedom and equality afforded women by the faith in most of the scriptures.

We are all one in Christ Jesus, and women and men alike are called to service and discipleship for their Lord. Thus, all that the scriptures have to say of that discipleship and service, all that is presupposed of and commanded for males, applies to females also. Husband and wife, male and female, stand before their Lord equally called, equally gifted with the Spirit, and equally responsible for using the gift.

About Children

One of the primary responsibilities that married people assume is the responsibility for the children that may result from their union. In this era of sexual permissiveness, easy contraception, and abortion on demand, that responsibility has often been carelessly cast aside, and our society and our children now are suffering the evil effects of such irresponsibility. But when two persons say "I do" at the altar, they are assuming the care of possible children, and no role given them is more important than that of parenthood, nor have they any greater influence on society than that rendered through their children's lives. As my wise Ph.D. adviser said to me in the second month of my first pregnancy, when I was busy with study and teaching and doctoral requirements, "Betty, if you don't do a good job with your children, you haven't done anything." God lets us share in his creative task of bringing forth and shaping new life by granting us the ability to "multiply" (Gen. 1:28). Surely no more awesome task has been entrusted to us!

It is true, children are not a necessity in the Christian home, according to the Bible. While Old Testament families understood barrenness as a curse of God (see Hos. 9:11–14; Isa. 4:1; 1 Sam. 1:1–18) because the only form of immortality known in Israel was the perpetuation of a man's name in his offspring, nevertheless Genesis 2:23–25 assumes that the marital union may be full and satisfying apart from the gift of children (but see Gen. 4:1). Similarly, the whole New Testament proclaims that our eternal life depends not on the perpetuation of the family name but on our faith in the resurrection of Jesus Christ. No barren couple need now believe that God is against them, and no responsible couple that chooses not to have children because of their particular situation (for example, in time of war) need guiltily feel that they are not serving their Lord.

Of course some couples do not have offspring for the most selfish reasons—because they simply do not want to be bothered, or because it would be inconvenient in their jobs, or even because the woman does not want to go through the strains and stresses and physical changes of pregnancy. How many abortions are performed for those selfish considerations! Other couples prevent all conceptions out of lack of faith. They do not want to bring children into a world like ours, forgetting that God is firmly in charge of our world; or they do not think they are "good enough" to raise children, forgetting that no one is good but God alone and that all of us are dependent on him to overcome our weaknesses, our errors, our lack of wisdom. It takes faith to bear and raise children properly—of that there is no doubt whatsoever. Nevertheless, the fact that children are not an absolute necessity in the Christian home is a freeing reality for some couples.

Children therefore come to us as a superfluity of God's grace. They are not a *sine qua non* for our lives. According to Genesis 1:28, they are the result of a special added blessing of God's—the frosting on our cake of matrimonial joy. And what a blessing they can be! Despite the fact that they totally change and disrupt our lives, despite the hours of work and care, of worry and frustration, of teaching and attention that they demand from us, they bring with them wondrous gifts, pressed down and overflowing: a new look at the world through their eyes; a reminder of our own past as children; participation in the future; and, above all else, the opportunity to shape and guide and teach a brand-new human being. I shall never forget the Easter Sunday I was carefully explaining to our four-year-old daughter at her bedtime that because Christ rose from the dead, we too could live eternally. Eyes filled with wonder, little face lighting up with joy, she exclaimed, "Mommy, I never knew that!" I had been given the rare opportunity to tell someone who had never understood it before about the gospel.

We parents learn a lot about ourselves from our children—that we are not perfect; that we get angry and impatient and tired; that we do not have all the wisdom we need to guide another's life, much less the life of the whole world; that we very much need forgiveness for our human errors and weaknesses. When I think of all the mistakes we made, especially with our firstborn, I am filled with gratitude for the grace of God that nevertheless guided that child and raised him up to be a fine human being. But we parents also learn from our children that we can be better than we thought—we can sacrifice sleep, time, material goods, and plans for the sake of another; we can love someone unfailingly who is acting totally unlovable; we can give ourselves away for the sake of another person and then find joy returned to us a hundredfold. The experience of raising children does, in truth, confirm our Lord's promise that whoever loses his life shall find it.

The scriptures do not say a lot about children, but what they do say is of utmost importance. Everywhere the love of parent for child is assumed in the Bible, so much so that the love of God can be compared to the love of a father (Ps. 103:13; Matt. 7:9–11) or of a mother (Isa. 49:15; 66:13). It is inconceivable, in biblical thought, that children are not cherished, and some of the most moving passages in the Bible portray the relations of parents and children (Gen. 22:1–19; 2 Sam. 18:33; Jer. 31:15; Mark 9:21–24; Luke 15:11–32).

The love of parent for child, in the biblical view, however, always includes within it discipline—that is, the training up of a child in the way he should go, so that "when he is old he will not depart from it" (Prov. 22:6). Parents are responsible for passing on to their children the knowledge of what is right and wrong; of what is valuable and lasting and what is worthless or transistory in human life; of what the limits of human life and action are; of proper roles in family and community and world; of responsibility to self and others and especially of responsibility to God; of how to use talents given in the service of others; of how to love and forgive and help.

In short, parents are responsible for passing on to children the Christian way of life. And that takes constant care and thought and the most intense kind of interest. When my own parents died, I realized that their interest had followed me all my life—that I had lost from my world the two people who cared to the depths of their beings what I was doing and what kind of person I was and what effect the world was having on me.

Christian parents, I think, have that interest from the day of their child's birth, and they are a different breed from those parents who are too busy or too tired or—God help us—too selfish to care what their children are doing and becoming. I cringe a little when some parent describes his or her child as a "free spirit." What that usually means is that the child has been left to grope along and find his own way, and far too often the way is one that leads to disaster. Proverbs 13:24 is out of date in its emphasis on corporal punishment, but its thought that those parents who neglect the discipline and training and guidance of their children are parents who really "hate" those children is a truth that is very much to the point.

Thus, throughout the scriptures, parents are admonished to discipline—that is, to train their children (Gen. 18:19; Prov. 19:18; 22:6; 29:15, 17; Eph. 6:4; Col. 3:21). So presupposed is this function of parenthood that it can be used as a metaphor of God's fatherly discipline of us (Deut. 8:5; 4:36; Prov. 3:11–12; Heb. 12:5–6). Similarly, children are admonished to listen to and obey the disciplining instruction of their parents (Prov. 1:8–9; 6:20; 10:1; Eph. 6:1–3; Col. 3:20), and this is understood as part of what it means to "honor" one's father and mother, as commanded in the Decalogue (Ex. 20:12; Deut. 5:16). Some parents perversely believe that they are "honoring" their children's personalities if they do not impose their views and values in any way on them. What they are really doing is abandoning their children to a world without structure, without meaning, without limits. Children are to honor their parents, according to the scriptures, and parents are to discipline and train their children. It is that proper, ordering, parent-child relationship that brings with it joy (see Prov. 29:17; 10:1; 15:20; 17:25), not to mention rest from worry and anxiety later on when the child has left home.

Parents, however, do not have unbridled freedom in raising their children, and this is the other important emphasis in the scriptures' understanding of this topic. "Fathers, do not provoke your children to anger," says Ephesians, "but bring them up in the discipline and instruction of the Lord" (Eph. 6:4; see also Col. 3:21). In other words, it is finally not our ways and views that we are to teach our children, for that would be to impose on them our prejudices, our fears, our hatreds, our sins and shortcomings. Far too many parents usurp the authority of God over their children's lives, insisting that their children grow up to do their will or fulfill their dreams or affirm their views. We have all observed such parents: the mother who constantly interferes in her married daughter's life; the father who insists that his son enroll in his alma mater or take up his career; the parents who have so smothered or manipulated their children with supposed "love" that the term has become a synonym for tyranny. We parents are not God; his thoughts are not our thoughts, and his ways are not our ways. And so the exhortation of the Bible is to bring up our children "in the discipline and instruction [nurture and admonition] of the Lord." Standing over our will and ways as parents are the will and ways of God, and all we do in relation to our children is to be measured against God's sovereign desire and character, as revealed to us through the scriptures. By that measure, our injustice and selfishness toward our children are exposed and can be corrected, just as by that measure our proper love and training of our children can be affirmed and sustained.

Teach your children what God has said and done: That is the constant admonition of Deuteronomy, the book of the Bible that discusses religious education more than does any other book. Diligently teach your children what God has commanded us to do (6:7; 11: 18–19), for by that teaching your children will know how to act in the world and you will be fulfilling your Lord's command to teach all nations, starting at home (Matt. 28:20). But also teach your children the long history of what God has done (4:9–10; 6:20–25; also Ps. 78:1–4)—for Christians not only the story of Israel in the Old Testament but also the story of Jesus Christ and the church in the New—for by that teaching your children will know who God is and what his goal and purpose for the world are. Then the children will have some meaning and purpose for their own living. Finally, says Deuteronomy, instruct and bring your children into the religious community of the covenant people (Deut. 31:10–13)—for Christians, into the church—for there children will fully learn who they really are, children of their heavenly Father (Gal. 4:6).

Our children really do not belong to us. They belong to God. They are his marvelous gifts, born out of the superfluity of his grace and entrusted to us to rear in the knowledge and obedience of him. Blessed are the children who can say that from childhood they have been acquainted by their parents with the sacred writings which are able to instruct them for salvation through faith in Christ Jesus (2 Tim. 3:15)!

About the Elderly

Our society does not usually regard someone as "old" until they have reached the age of 75 or 80, or until they have become infirm. We have lots of retirees who lead vigorous, comfortable, and interesting lives as fully accepted members of society. While the stereotype still persists in some quarters that a person has worth only as long as he or she can produce, it is rapidly giving way before booming businesses in education, travel, recreation, housing, and culture for our older citizens. Indeed, many churches have learned to use the skills and experience of their older members, who have free time, on committees and national boards.

Thus, the biblical view that a "good old age" (Gen. 15:15; 25:8; Judg. 8:32; 1 Chron. 29:28) or a "ripe old age" (Job 5:26) is a desirable state can be echoed by many. When Third Isaiah pictures the kingdom of God come on earth, it says that there will not be in it "an old man who does not fill out his days" (Isa. 65: 20), just as Zechariah proclaims that "old men and old women shall again sit in the streets of Jerusalem, each with staff in hand for very age" (8:4). The elderly were sometimes valued for their wisdom in Israel (see John

8:9), serving as advisers to kings (2 Chron. 10:6–7) and judges in the lay courts (Lam. 5:14), examples that could find analogies in our contemporary governments. Old age was to be respected among the covenant people (see Prov. 20:29), and Isaiah of Jerusalem considered it a sign of chaos in society when the youth was insolent to the elder (Isa. 3:5). Thus 1 Timothy instructs the church, "Do not rebuke an older man but exhort him as you would a father; treat younger men like brothers, older women like mothers, younger women like sisters, in all purity" (1 Tim. 5:1–2).

Nevertheless, the infirmities of old age are known to most of us in our later years. As Golda Meir wrote in her autobiography, "It is not a sin to be 70 but it is also no joke." And when still later years are reached, they often can become a time of gradually narrowing horizons. Physical vision literally narrows, with loss of peripheral sight and the growth of cataracts. Steps become less sure, travel more difficult. Friends pass away, and new friends are harder to make. Invitations become less frequent; social horizons narrow. Older persons are driven more and more back into themselves. As a friend put it in a Christmas letter, "Nearing the end of the road, time seems to accelerate, space shrinks, past shifts nearer, future turns into present too quickly, five-day-old memories tend to fade whereas the fifty-year-oldies glow with clarity."[2] That which happens to the older person takes place more and more in the mind, and memory of the past can crowd out awareness and interest in the present and future.

The Bible—that realistic book—is aware of these developments as well. It knows that the elderly can be anything but wise (Job 32:9; Eccl. 4:13), that they can be diseased (1 Kings 15:23), that physical strength fails (Ps. 71:9; see also Hos. 7:9), and that old age can leave one helpless and dependent (see John 21:18). The picture of the aged David in 1 Kings 1:1–4 is probably as telling a portrayal as was ever written.

Certainly there is fear that surrounds such realities for our elderly, not so much fear of death—that can even be welcome—but the fear of becoming helpless and dependent. One prominent churchman and his wife committed suicide rather than face that helplessness, and many an elderly soul has prayed for death to come soon enough.

There is also the fear of becoming a caricature of one's former self, of having some long-hidden characteristic take over one's personality, of becoming like one of the types seen in nursing homes: the worrier, the whiner, the self-righteous scold, the hermit, the frightened, the exhibitionist, the miser. Out of control, the aged can reveal their hidden selves, and who knows what personalities lurk in the depths of our ids? And so perhaps the prayer of the psalmist is the prayer of all of us:

> . . . thou, O Lord, art my hope . . .
> Do not cast me off in the time of old age;
>   forsake me not when my strength is spent.
> (Psalm 71:5, 9)

Certainly the scriptures demand that honor for our parents never cease. "Hearken to your father who begot you, and do not despise your mother when she is old," advises Proverbs 23:22, and there are no conditions attached to that wisdom. The father, no matter how foolish, is to be heard and acknowledged; the mother, no matter her physical and mental condition, is to be cherished and not despised.

But the scriptures go far beyond that in assurance given to the elderly. First of all, God never forsakes those of faith:

> Hearken to me, O house of Jacob,
>   all the remnant of the house of Israel,
> who have been borne by me from your birth,
>   carried from the womb;
> even to your old age I am He,

and to gray hairs I will carry you.
I have made, and I will bear;
    I will carry and will save.
                    (Isaiah 46:3–4)

This God of the Bible is a God who has led us all our
life long (Gen. 48:15) and who is with us and will keep
us and never leave us until he has done all that of
which he has spoken to us (Gen. 28:15; see also Phil.
1:6). Therefore the faithful elderly can fill out their
days, knowing that nothing can separate them from
the love and purpose of such a God (see Rom. 8:38–
39). God has a reason for our lives, even if we are 85,
and he carefully watches over us and guides us.

In fact, all that the scriptures say about the purpose
and presence of God in the midst of suffering, about
the plan of God for our living, about his call to us to
trust in him and his working—nothing of that suddenly ceases to be applicable when we reach retire-
ment age. Residents of homes for the elderly are
sometimes heard to complain that visiting clergy
never preach to them the full gospel but instead often
"talk down" to them or offer them only cheap and
undemanding comfort. But that is not the case in the
scriptures. Discipleship, vigorous trust, service of God
to the extent of ability in the Spirit—these are still
expected of those elderly who believe in the Lord. As
Malcolm Cowley has said in his book *The View from
Eighty*, it is still the elderly's "duty to share affection
and contribute to the world as much as possible."[3]
The letter to Titus puts it much more fully:

> Bid the older men be temperate, serious, sensible,
> sound in faith, in love, and in steadfastness. Bid the
> older women likewise to be reverent in behavior . . . ;
> they are to teach what is good, . . . that the word of God
> may not be discredited. (Titus 2:2–5)

Until our minds and therefore responsibility go, we
are called to serve the Lord.

Perhaps that can be emphasized by reading Psalm 92 as a song of thanksgiving sung by an elderly person. This psalm is not the expression of a feeble and helpless old man, clucking his tongue over the terrible ways of modern society. This is the song of one who knows that God rules the world and that no evil will thwart God's good purpose; who, though feeble himself, finds his strength in God; and who therefore finds himself flourishing (vs. 12–14) and full of joy (v. 4) in his Lord. He may be bedridden, but he can still give thanks to his God and rejoice in the works of God's hands. Some writers counsel that old age is the time to find and know yourself. For example, Vera Scott-Maxwell has written, "If at the end of your life you have only yourself, it is much."[4] Perhaps that is true. But the singer of Psalm 92 has found and knows much more—namely, the strength and faithfulness of his God. Wrote my friend who had just celebrated her fiftieth wedding anniversary, "We could not have survived our fifty years . . . without learning and learning and relearning 'to know whom we believed.' "[5]

Lord, "so teach us to number our days that we may get a heart of [such] wisdom" (Ps. 90:12).

5

Speaking the Truth in Love

We have a fairly clear idea now of what the Bible says about a number of subjects connected with home life, and we have explored the condition of the society with which our people have to contend as they try to live as Christian families. In addition, we have discussed some of the presuppositions that the biblical faith brings to that attempt. Now we are confronted with the question, How can we preach the biblical message in such an age as ours? How can a homiletician stand up in the pulpit and talk about God's good gift of marriage, when he or she knows that so many marriages in the congregation are hurting? How can the preacher speak of God's hatred of divorce, when so many divorced men and women look back from the pews? How can the intention of God for home life be proclaimed when we are so far from fulfilling that intention?

These are questions that confront the preacher with the tension that exists between his or her role as a pastor and as a prophet. As prophets—that is, as bearers of the Word of God—we preachers are called faithfully to proclaim not the message of our culture, and not our own opinions, but the gospel that has been handed on to us in the scriptures by the church. We are stewards of the mysteries of God, Paul tells us, and "it is required of stewards that they be found trustworthy" (1 Cor. 4:1–2)—that they do not neglect or spoil or dilute the Word of God entrusted to them. On the other hand, as pastors we are equally called to shepherd our sheep—to seek the lost, feed the hungry, comfort the fearful, bind up the wounds of the hurting. And it sometimes seems to us that to announce the clear Word of God—for example, with respect to divorce—would be to do nothing but rub salt in the wounds. Yet, if the gospel is in fact good news and not bad, there should be some resolution possible of the tension between our roles as pastors and as prophets of the Word of God.

First of all, let it be said that the pulpit of the Christian church should never be allowed to find itself in the situation of always simply reacting to crises in the life of a congregation. To be in that situation is suddenly to spring a message on a congregation that they have never heard before and are totally unprepared to receive. Worst of all, it can have the effect of singling out the persons in the pews who are having problems, and that is a breach of pastoral confidentiality and a disrespect for persons that is unforgivable in the preacher.

Rather, preaching about family life to a congregation requires such preaching be set in the context of an ongoing program in the total life of the congregation. The Sunday school, from nursery on up, should include considerations of Christian home life in its curriculum. Youth groups should discuss, in depth, sexuality and marriage and family life and their responsibilities. Marriage enrichment programs may be held on congregational retreats from time to time. Films at church-night suppers, special speakers and programs that utilize counseling and mental health resources in the area, follow-up programs for the newly wed, church celebrations of anniversaries, regular premarital counseling on the part of the pastor, and instruction at times of baptism and confirmation—all can and should form a context and support for preaching. From such a total program of the church, congregational members will learn that their family concerns and problems are neither being singled out nor attacked from the pulpit, but that the church of Christ has an ongoing concern for the family well-being of its members. Moreover, such a total program will furnish a background of understanding for the proclamation from the pulpit, as well as give ample opportunity for discussion of all those complicated details and questions that cannot be thoroughly treated in a twenty-minute sermon. Perhaps the lack of such a total program in many congregations forms another reason why so many preachers do not deal with family concerns from the pulpit. But surely in our time, in which so many of our homes are crumbling and thus threatening the very life of our nation, that is a lack which we and our people truly cannot afford.

Let it be said, second, that our people need to hear the truth. We do them no favor if, in some sort of misguided attempt to make either our ministry or the Bible more acceptable to them, we hide the truth of what the scriptures really say. There is no easy accommodation to be had between the world's ways and the Christian way, and those prophets who try to identify the one with the other are repeatedly condemned as false prophets in the Bible (see Jer. 6:13–15; 23:16–22; Ezek. 13; Zech. 10:2).

If our people never hear preached to them God's intention for our homes, how will they know what God's will is for their lives? And apart from hearing that Word, how can they know what their Creator expects them to do? We cannot just abandon them to the world and to themselves. That would be to leave them "harassed and helpless, like sheep without a shepherd" (Matt. 9:36; Mark 6:34; see also Num. 27: 17), to make them like rudderless boats, "tossed to and fro and carried about with every wind of doctrine" (Eph. 4:14). If we truly believe—truly believe—that the will of God is mediated to us through the scriptures and that the scriptures are our authority for faith and practice, and if we really trust that we have been called to proclaim the Word of God to our people, then we can do no other than let our congregations know, fully and truthfully, what the scriptures say about their family concerns. To do less would be to deny to our people the abundant life that our Lord promises we can inherit by trust in him, the incarnate Word.

We sometimes get surprising reactions to sermons that fully explicate the Word of God. There is a hunger on the part of many people in our congregations to know what the Bible says about their everyday living. They truly do want to know! They hunger and thirst for someone to preach with authority from the scriptures, and far too often they go away disappointed.

It has also been my experience that many in a congregation will react to a sermon on marriage as the good gift of God, for example, with an expression of relief and joy. They have heard for so long from the media that Christian marriage is an impossibility, or that faithful marriage is passé, that when someone comes bearing the good news of marriage their reaction is one of gratitude. *Finally* someone has affirmed what these people have experienced in their homes— that marriage and home life, for all their trauma, are gracious gifts of a loving Lord. And their reaction to hearing that good news is thanksgiving to God for the gifts. We need to affirm the Christian marriages that are in fact found among the members in most of our congregations.

Even those persons in a congregation who have no real faith and who do not believe the Word are usually alienated further from the gospel by the preacher who tries to dilute it or to accommodate it to society's views. Even the unbelieving know when a preacher is hedging! When our daughter was in college, she reported that the college chaplain was secretly laughed at and openly ignored by most of the students, because he repeatedly sanctioned student immorality rather than speak any word of judgment. The students knew they were being conned, and they scorned the deceit involved. Such temporizing preachers should remember that through all the student rebellions of the '60s and '70s, and despite all the permissiveness of our time, the one figure that is never put down, even by the most rebellious in our society, is the figure of Jesus. Some persons may not follow him, but they do not call him a phony. And we preachers are the servants of that authentic Man, called to proclaim his gospel in integrity and truth.

One also has to ask if it is not the truth of the Bible that allows our people to feel that their actual lives are being dealt with from the pulpit. For example, when God says through his prophet Malachi, "I hate divorce" (2:16), does that attitude not deal with the reality of the breakup of a home—the awful sense of failure that accompanies so many divorces, the panic of suddenly being on one's own, the trauma inflicted on the children, the tears, the loneliness, the angers, the regrets, sometimes even the guilty relief? Are those not all hateful experiences that the divorcing go through? And is it not finally a manifestation of the mercy of God that he hates such results also? Surely if God is a loving Father, he suffers over every hurt inflicted on his children, and he does indeed hate what that hurt does to their lives and the lives of their offspring.

This is finally the truth of the scriptures—that they are so realistic, for immediately after the joyful picture in Genesis 2:24 of husband and wife become one flesh in the new community of matrimony, the disruption of that community by our sin is pictured, in Genesis 3. The scriptures know all about our failures. When the man and his wife try to become their own gods, when they disobey the commandment of their Lord and try to shape their own lives and futures, their joyful unity of one flesh is broken, and they become naked, self-enclosed egos, standing over against one another in shame, refusing to take responsibility for one another and for their sin. "Then the eyes of both were opened," Genesis puts it, "and they knew that they were naked" (v. 7). So we have the picture of you and me trying to pass the buck: "The woman whom thou gavest to be with me, she gave me fruit of the tree, and I ate" (v. 12)—"Lord, it's not my fault; it's hers, or yours!" And from the woman, "The serpent beguiled me, and I ate" (v. 13)—"Lord, I live in an evil environment." But the realism continues; God holds us responsible for our rebellion against his will: "What is this that you have done?" he asks (v. 13). So the judgment that is laid on the original couple—who really stand for you and me—the judgment is that no longer will they know a joyful unity of love, but only the battle of the sexes. "Your desire shall be for your husband," the woman is told, "and he shall rule over you" (v. 16). Now the marital relation is disrupted by that humiliating domination against which the women's movement has raised its voice in our time in an agonized cry. The battle of the sexes and the inferiority of women, Genesis says, are the result of our sin, just as our broken marriages, our tortured homes, our terribly disrupted marital relations are the result of our refusal to let God be Lord over our lives.

That picture of marriage and family under judgment is really what our culture thinks home life is like now—that there is no possibility of having a faithful, lifelong, happy marital union. No, says our society, everything is distorted now, with little misunderstandings and wounds inflicted, and the inability of husbands and wives to speak the words that reveal anything of their hearts. And there is no healing for it all. As in T. S. Eliot's play *The Family Reunion:*

> There is no avoiding these things
> And we know nothing of exorcism . . .

There are certain inflexible laws
Unalterable, in the nature of music.
There is nothing at all to be done about it,
There is nothing to do about anything.[1]

But there *is* something to be done about it, because
the most realistic fact about the scriptures is that they
know, in contradiction to the views of our society, that
God has not deserted us. We have always to reckon
with that God of mercy. He may hate what our sin has
done to us and to our homes. He has always to contend with our "hardness of heart" (Mark 10:5 and
par.). He may grieve over our failures and follies and
faithlessness (cf. Hos. 11:8). But the final fact is that
he will not abandon us to the ruin that our sin brings
upon us. And so, in Jesus Christ, God does something
about it.

In the first place, he overcomes the split, the ancient
feud between male and female, and now in Christ
there is no more battle of the sexes. Of course that
battle is partly a battle over power—over the question
of who is going to exercise final authority in a home—
and there can be no satisfactory home life until that
issue is settled. As Dr. Jerry M. Lewis has said, "In
healthy families, parents have shared power"; they
have resolved the issue of "how to make decisions and
resolve disagreements in a way that is satisfactory to
both partners."[2] And the scriptures tell us that is ex-
actly what God in Christ provides for us—shared
power. "There is neither male nor female" any more,
no domination of one by the other, "for you are all
one in Christ Jesus" (Gal. 3:28). Both husband and
wife are mutually subject one to the other "out of
reverence [obedience] for Christ" (Eph. 5:21). Power
shifts back and forth, each partner exercises authority,
in the oneness and respect that they have for each
other, under the lordship of Christ. God in his Son has
overcome the effect of our sinful attempt to be our
own gods, and it is now possible to reclaim that joyful

unity of one flesh that God intended for our marital unions from the beginning.

Second, because God in Christ has triumphed over the evil power of this world that nailed him to a cross, it is now possible to be free of our captivity to the ways of our sinful society. We no longer need to be children tossed to and fro by every wind of doctrine. We no longer need to be slaves of sin, following every fad or folly that our society sets forth about home life. Now we are slaves of Jesus Christ. He has made us his own. God has bought us with the redemption price of his beloved Son, and we no longer need to be conformed to this world and its transitory and corrupted ways. In Christ, we have begun to inherit the glorious liberty of the children of God, and by God's grace it is now possible to have a Christian home.

Third, because God in Christ has poured out his Spirit upon us, it is now possible in our family life to exercise powers of forgiveness and faithfulness and love far beyond our own feeble abilities to create and sustain them. The New Testament sets forth a fantastic model for our marital union. In Ephesians 5:21–32, it says that the love we have for one another in our marriages is to be the earthly, visible symbol of Christ's love for his church. In other words, when our neighbors and friends look at our marriages, they are to see the love of God in his Son—that love which would not let us go; which poured itself forth in giving, even to death on the cross; which remains faithfully with us though the powers of evil rage against it. Nothing can separate us from that love of Christ, and so nothing is to separate Christian marital partners either. The love we have for one another in our homes is to reflect the constancy and the self-sacrifice of Christ.

Who lives up to that in marriage? Measured against the love of God in Jesus Christ, we all fall short and are wanting. And the prayer of every Christian, whether married or divorced, whether old or young,

whether single or separated, can only start with that
repentant plea, "Lord, be merciful to me, a sinner."
Divorced persons in our congregations sometimes
find themselves shunned in the church, as if they were
pariahs or as if somehow they were the only sinners,
polluting an otherwise perfect body of married saints.
But we should stop deceiving ourselves in our
pharisaic self-righteousness. No one of us, in our
home life, has lived up to the love of God. We all have
sinned and fallen short of the faithfulness of Jesus. In
Hosea's thought, we all are harlots, breaking marriage
covenant with God and with one another. We all participate in sin. We all are equally guilty.

We cannot rely on our own righteousness in our
marriages and homes, any more than we can rely on
it in any other relationship. We do not have the power
within ourselves to create a Christian marriage of joy
and fidelity and trust, any more than we have that
power to create those qualities within a church or a
society or a nation. If you and I are simply on our own,
then we can never live up to our Christian wedding
vows: to have and to hold from this day forward, for
better, for worse, for richer, for poorer, in sickness
and in health, to love and to cherish till death does us
part. Those are impossible vows, as our sinful society
knows they are impossible, if by our strength and
faithfulness we are to keep them simply on our own.

But we are not on our own. That is the Christian
gospel. We are not on our own but joined together in
holy matrimony according to God's holy ordinance,
and therefore held together and sustained in our life
together by the love and power of God in Christ,
poured out to us by the Spirit. He has saved us not
only as individuals but also as husbands and wives and
fathers and mothers. And he works in our marriages
and homes beyond all our power to work and to make
them whole.

When we have no more power in our marriage to

forgive, Christ can heal our conflict. When we are at our selfish, unlovable worst, he nevertheless can sustain our love for one another. When we are most weak and tempted by the siren song of our sinful society, he can hold the bonds of faithfulness firm by his unswerving devotion. And out of all that loving care with which Christ works in our wedded unions, there can in fact be forged a home life together against which the very powers of hell cannot prevail, and which lasts and lasts till death does us part, in joy and fidelity and goodness. "O the depth of the riches and wisdom and knowledge of God!" (Rom. 11:33). With what love he has loved us in Jesus Christ, also in our homes and families!

Fourth, because God in Jesus Christ has forgiven us our sins and triumphed over them in the resurrection, our failures in our marital and home relationships are no longer the last word. Despite the grace poured out on us, sufficient for all our needs, we do in fact fail. Homes fall apart and marriages end in divorce courts, just as children go astray and relationships with siblings and parents and elderly turn sour.

No Christian can confront such failures without a deep sense of responsibility and repentance for corrupting the good gifts that God has given him or her. "Guilt" is not a popular word in our time, and preachers sometimes hesitate to lay upon their people the Word of God that will make them feel remorse. But let's face it: We are guilty. All of us are guilty. All of us distort and corrupt the gracious gifts our Creator has given us. Nevertheless, the glad news of the Christian gospel is that there is a new beginning. "Behold, I make all things new," our Creator tells us (Rev. 21:5). "If anyone is in Christ, he is a new creation; the old has passed away, behold, the new has come" (2 Cor. 5:17). There is no sin, no failure, no wrong that cannot be forgiven by the cross and resurrection of Jesus Christ. And for all who trust him with their lives, there is new hope, a new beginning, and the possibility of a new life, lived according to the intention of God in the power of his Spirit.

We can speak the truth to our congregations about their family concerns from our pulpits, because the truth of the scriptures is given us in love. "I say that we are wound with mercy round and round, as if with air"[3]—with the mercy of a Savior who is determined that we shall have life and have it more abundantly; with the love of a God whose Word is always finally good news and not bad; with the never-failing compassion of a Lord who has triumphed over all our failures. Surely to deny our people such a gospel and to fail to speak to them its truth in love would be to prove unworthy of the calling to which in fact we have been called.

There are two further facts with regard to family concerns that the preacher needs to impress on his or her congregation, however, and these have to do with Christian discipleship and witness. Our people are so accustomed to separating their home life from their Christian faith, and so convinced by our culture that family concerns have nothing to do with what they believe, that it sometimes happens that a couple will participate in the communion—the fellowship, the unifying act of the Lord's Supper—in church at 11 A.M. on Sunday, and yet refuse to speak to one another for the rest of the day, because they have had a fight at the breakfast table. Or there are spouses who pray every Sunday, "Forgive us our debts as we forgive our debtors," and yet who nourish grudges against one another as they sit in their living room. Or there are couples who will "pass the peace" at church and never realize that it is incumbent on them first of all to pass it to one another. Thus, when there is serious trouble in a relationship and a couple is considering separation, they will ask every question except the most important one. The questions always are: Will I be happier? Will it be better for the children? Can I make it on my own? But never: Is this separation the will of God for our lives? Our home life has become thoroughly secularized—that is, we think God is absent from it—and so we have turned for guidance to the experts and counselors and psychologists. Or we have let our society's ideas about home life influence our decisions, and slowly, inexorably, those sick ideas are undermining our families.

But Christians are people who acknowledge the lordship of Jesus Christ over the whole of their faith and practice, and preachers need to stress that lordship in relation to the family. For example, all of us know that we are commanded by our Lord to love our neighbors as ourselves. But we fail to realize what Luther once pointed out, that the nearest and dearest neighbor is the mate with whom we live, and it is there, in our living rooms and bedrooms and dining rooms, that our discipleship must begin. We can deny Jesus Christ as surely over our breakfast tables as we can in our neglect of prayer and worship. Or, conversely, we can serve him as fully in our day-to-day reactions to our marital partners as we can in our activities on behalf of the poor.

It is precisely this thought which that great passage on marriage in Ephesians 5:21–33 sets forth. Husbands and wives, says the author of Ephesians, are to be subject to one another "out of reverence for Christ." In short, what we do to our spouses in our homes is what we are doing to our Lord. The passage might have paraphrased the familiar words of Jesus, "Inasmuch as you have done it unto one of the least of these—your mate—you have done it unto me" (Matt. 25:40, kjv). Wives are to love their husbands as if they were the Lord. Husbands are to love their wives as if they were Christ's body, the church. In both cases, how we act toward one another in our marriages is action toward Jesus Christ. Neglect or anger or faith-

lessness toward a spouse is done toward the Master we
are called to serve. And fidelity, service, love in our
homes are rendered to God in his Son.

It can make all the difference in the world for a
family to realize that they have to do not just with one
another but always also with God. A troubled woman
came to me, asking if she should divorce her husband,
who had been cool to her because she had been left
slightly crippled in one leg by a stroke. When I
pointed out to her, after we had thoroughly discussed
the situation, that she had to make such a decision in
the light of her relationship with God, she immediately
rejected all thought of divorce and decided she could
improve the relationship. "I certainly don't want to
get into trouble with God!" were her words. Preachers
need to impress on their congregations that finally we
have to do with the Lord, and if that relationship is
realized, family concerns take on a new context and
perspective. They are lent a new motive power which
they do not possess in themselves.

To go further, every Christian in the church is called
to be a witness for the Lord. "You are my witnesses,"
God proclaimed to the covenant people (Isa. 43:10,
12; 44:8), just as he named his disciples to be his
witnesses "to the end of the earth" (Acts 1:8): witnesses to the truth in Christ (John 15:27), witnesses to
all that Christ did (Acts 10:39), witnesses to his life and
death and resurrection (Luke 24:48; Acts 2:32; 3:15;
5:32; 13:31). In fact, God specifically chose every
Christian to be the witness of his victory in Christ over
sin and death (Acts 10:41; Heb. 12:1). And our family
life is to be a part of that witness.

It is strange what powerful testimony our relationships in our homes render to other people. Said one
woman angrily to a close friend who had just gotten
a divorce, "Stop threatening my marriage!" And that's
the way we all feel when we watch the marriage of a
friend or relative fall apart—that somehow our homes
are threatened too, as if some mysterious power of evil

had won a victory and were now going to turn on us. And so we try to draw into our little home circle more tightly to ward off the attack. The foundations of our lives seem shaken when someone else's home fails, and perhaps that is another reason why divorced persons sometimes find themselves shunned. Their failure seems a sign of the fact that an evil force is loose in the world, and so we sometimes selfishly try to protect ourselves from it by ostracizing the divorced. It is not a Christian reaction, of course, because God in Christ has won the victory over all evil, and we are called to minister to those who suffer and are hurting. Nevertheless, this is an illustration of how powerfully our home life affects others.

Thus, every Christian must ask himself or herself what testimony some act in the home will make to the Lord. Will an act give the witness that God is impotent or will it testify to his victory in Christ? For example, what witness did that aged couple mentioned in chapter 4, who committed suicide rather than face a nursing home, give to every other elderly person? That God was no longer sufficient? That he had no further purpose for their lives? Or that they were lords over their own lives and deaths? In one way, it may seem callous to raise such questions, but in another, those are always proper questions for the Christian, for we are in fact responsible for the testimony about God that our lives and actions are giving to other persons. We are surrounded in the communion of saints by a cloud of faithful witnesses, and so we are to "lay aside every weight, and sin which clings so closely," and we are to "run with perseverance the race that is set before us, looking to Jesus," whose life, even unto death on the cross, bore testimony to the power and love of God (Heb. 12:1–2).

There is a further thought that we should consider in relation to our personal responsibility to be witnesses in our home life for God: It is now time to make a practice of sharing our satisfactions. On every hand, our society is telling us that a faithfully happy, lifelong marital relationship is impossible, and our young people have been so overwhelmed by that cynicism that many of them are now afraid to get married. Thousands of us, however, know that Christian marriage is in fact possible, and thousands of us rejoice in a wedded unity of fidelity and joy and purpose. To be sure, all such unions have their ups and downs. As one wise woman expressed it, "Love is what you have gone through together." Countless couples in the church know the joyful truth of that.

The difficulty is that we are very quiet about the satisfactions and personal growth and happiness that our home relations afford us. We enjoy them, and we celebrate them in the privacy of our own families, but we do not say very much about them to other people.

The time has now come to speak. It is no longer enough to keep our family joys to ourselves. It is no longer enough simply to *be.* Now, in the face of the attacks taking place against marriage and the home in the United States, it is time for words. It is time for the proclamation that Christian marriage is indeed a possibility and a reality in our homes. It is time to let that be known in our churches and neighborhoods, and among our friends, and above all among our children and grandchildren. It is time to celebrate every marriage anniversary and to protest every media attack against the home. In short, it is time to obey the words of our Lord in the Sermon on the Mount, "Let your light so shine before men, that they may see your good works, and give glory to your Father who is in heaven." It is time to apply that to our family life—to let the light of our homes shine forth, to set our lamps on a stand, that they may give light to all others in their homes (Matt. 5:14–16).

There are comfort and strength lent to other persons by the existence of a Christian home. One year a daughter sent a card to her parents on their thirty-fourth wedding anniversary, with a note attached.

"Thank you," it said, "for showing me what a marriage can be." How many of our offspring hunger and thirst to be shown what a Christian marriage and home can be! When any faithful couple persevere in their love of God and one another through trouble and trials, through heartaches and disappointments, through sickness and health, through struggles and successes, this perseverance proclaims to all who know them that there is a transcendent power of God that carries them and empowers their love and sustains their home beyond all their own power to sustain it. The Christian home often is, with Paul, "afflicted in every way, but not crushed; perplexed, but not driven to despair; . . . struck down, but not destroyed" (2 Cor. 4:8–9), because it lives by God's power and not by its own. And that is the testimony that now needs to be given in the midst of our despairing and cynical society. We can paraphrase the text from Matthew to call for such testimony: Let the light of your home life so shine before others, that they may see the good works that Jesus Christ works in you, and give glory to your Father who is in heaven.

6

Using Other Texts and Illustrations

We have now discussed or alluded to most of the texts in the Bible that have directly to do with family concerns, and we have used some texts, such as Matthew 5:14–16, that seem not so directly related to those concerns. It is the latter practice that we wish to discuss further in this chapter.

There are many passages in the Bible that do not directly discuss family matters and yet that can be applied to family life. In fact, there are almost no biblical texts that cannot be applied to family life, because the whole of the Christian faith bears on the way we relate to one another in our homes, just as it bears on everything we do and say in our neighborhoods and society and world. But perhaps it would be helpful to single out some specific biblical passages and show their relation to home life.

Philippians 2:12–13

Let us consider, first of all, Philippians 2:12–13: "Work out your own salvation with fear and trembling; for God is at work in you, both to will and to work for his good pleasure." Few texts are more applicable than this one to Christian marriage. The gospel holds before us the possibility of having a lifelong, faithfully happy Christian marriage, but as with every promise given us by the gospel, we have to seize that possibility. The Christian life is not a matter of simply floating down the stream of grace—of expecting God to give us gifts for which we do not eagerly and expectantly work every day. No, we must work out our own salvation. We must want a Christian marriage so much that we are willing to expend the most strenuous efforts to achieve it. And every harmoniously married couple knows just how strenuous and unremitting those efforts must be. We should never look at a happily married couple and think how lucky they are to be so happy. Behind their concord is the most strenuous achievement.

Thus, the preacher has an opportunity in relation to this text to deal with some of the tasks in marriage that a couple has to work at: communicating with one another, solving money problems, arriving at common values, agreeing on child-raising techniques, dealing from a united front with in-laws, resolving conflicts and anger. Such tasks can either be treated very specifically by the preacher or be used as general illustrations of the effort necessary to claim God's intention for marriage. But all these tasks should be discussed within the Christian perspective and on the basis of those biblical presuppositions that we dealt with in chapter 3. The first part of the message, however, is that we are called in our homes to the most strenuous discipleship—indeed, to a strenuous discipleship that never ends until death does us part, for a couple's personalities and circumstances are constantly changing, and every change brings with it new tasks and adjustments.

The good news then follows from the rest of the text. Midst all our striving, our work, our efforts at understanding and forgiving and sharing, the God of love is at work to make of our marriages and homes that which he intends them to be. We are not on our own, alone in the world, struggling desperately to win our own happiness. A God is at work who wills that we have life together and have it more abundantly. All our efforts finally find their motive power, their sustenance, their guidance, and their fulfillment through our trust in God. And by that trust, it is not finally we who work but Jesus Christ who works in us. The text takes on concrete meaning when applied to marriage, just as it lends to marriage the ultimate assurance of the gospel.

Galatians 3:23–24

Very similar in some of its application to marriage is the text from Galatians 3:23–24: "Now before faith came, we were confined under the law, kept under restraint until faith should be revealed. So that the law was our custodian until Christ came, that we might be justified by faith." There are probably few texts that make less sense to our congregations than do Paul's discussions of the law in Galatians and in Romans. It all seems so abstract to our people, and so totally irrelevant. But if we apply this text from Galatians 3 to the marital relationship, it suddenly begins to take on meaning.

Suppose we are dealing with fidelity in marriage. How is it that the Christian marriage really can be held together? What is it that keeps us gladly faithful until the day of our death? Surely it is not the fact that we have a marriage license or that we made certain promises at the time of our wedding. The practices of our society are ample evidence that no legality can assure the constancy of a marriage bond.

And yet, so many Christian couples do not realize the fact that the law has no power to save—that is, to give vitality and joy to their wedded union. Good church members that they are, they hear the biblical condemnations of divorce and adultery, and they apply those biblical teachings to their own marriages in the form of law. They naively assume that because they are Christians, they will obey the law and will never be unfaithful, and very often they therefore cease to make any effort to resolve their conflicts and to deepen their relationship. It has been discovered by marital counselors that most couples perceive their relationship to be less and less satisfactory as the years go on, and one of the reasons is that the relationship is simply taken for granted. Christian couples assume that the legality of their relationship is sufficient to nurture it, when in fact the law has no power whatsoever to give us life, as Paul says in this text. Such couples may remain together, from a legal point of view, but in actuality their life together ended many years before. It is not the law that holds a marriage together.

The law is, however, not to be viewed in totally negative terms. In Romans 7:12, Paul supplements this Galatians text by writing that "the law is holy, and the commandment is holy and just and good." And in the text from Galatians he states that "the law was our custodian until Christ came." What do those two statements mean?

Certainly any thoughtful and sincere Christian spouse knows what it is to be grateful for the law. There are times in the lives of all of us when we have been sorely tried, when we know very well that our marriage has been held together by little more than duty, when obligation to legalistic expectation has prevented us from taking a foolish course of action that we undoubtedly would have grievously regretted later on. When temptation comes, as it comes in any marriage, it is good to know in the back of our minds that stern and divine "Thou shalt not . . ."! The law can, as Paul says, act as a check on our sin. It is, in the words of our text, our custodian until Christ comes.

But truly joyful marriages are never built on codes and legalistic contracts alone, and those modern couples who are writing out detailed marriage contracts with one another these days need to learn that fact. Neither are truly satisfying marriages held together by social convention, or for the sake of the children, or for economic reasons, or for convenience.

Rather, in marriage as in every other sphere, we are justified by faith alone. Our trust and commitment alone can mediate wholeness to us. We trust one another and we commit ourselves to one another in marriage, and we thereby know the freedom fully to reveal ourselves to one another. But above all, in Christian marriage we trust Jesus Christ and commit ourselves to him. We know that it is finally only his life and death and resurrection that make a true and joyful union of one flesh possible. We know that it is only in the power of his love that we have the possibility truly to love and forgive and honor one another.

We commit ourselves to Christ. And so we try in our marriages to follow his commands, because we know that he desires that we have fullness of life, and we trust that his commands will show us the way to walk and to grow up into that fullness. "These things I have spoken to you, that my joy may be in you, and that your joy may be full" (John 15:11). Christ's command comes to us not as some law but as words to lead us into the fullness of joy, as continual merciful guidance in the relationship that he has in fact made possible between husband and wife.

We commit ourselves to Christ. And so in gratitude and love to him, we try to walk in relation to one another as Christ has walked with us—in forgiveness, in service, in faithfulness, in humility and understanding. We commit ourselves in Christian marriage to the imitation of Christ's love for us (cf. Eph. 5:1), and that commitment involves a constant willing and working, a day-by-day necessity of taking the time and trouble to care.

There are, to be sure, many times in Christian marriage when we can walk only by faith and not by sight. There are periods in the life of every couple when all seems hopeless and ruined, when conflict and misunderstanding and betrayal dominate the home, when it seems as if our relationship can never be whole and joyful again, and we are tempted to think that God did not intend it in the beginning.

Then, above all other times, is the time when we trust—trust that God had a purpose in bringing us together as a couple, trust in the power of the cross of Christ to overcome our division and evil, trust in the power of the resurrection of Christ to make even our marriage new. Such trust does not guarantee an instant miracle, to be sure. It does, however, lead one to know that with God all things are possible. And in such trust and knowledge, very often the possible becomes reality.

We are justified by faith, not by the law. Trust and commitment to our Lord and to one another hold together a Christian marriage and give it its permanence, its uniqueness, its marvelous joy.

Mark 12:28–30

In relation to the roles of male and female in marriage, the preacher could use the great commandment of Jesus, which comes to us originally from Deuteronomy 6:4 and then is repeated in a slightly expanded form by Jesus, according to Mark 12:28–30: "You shall love the Lord your God with all your heart, and with all your soul, and with all your mind, and with all your strength." This text is not often applied to marriage, but its application in that context can make it very specific.

For years, females in American society have been denied the full development of their personhood, and while great strides have been made in opening opportunities to women, our society still recoils somewhat from women who use their minds. The woman who speaks out in a group, who argues a cause, who joins men in a discussion at a party is still regarded as "pushy." The stereotype of woman as the one who stays home and cooks and raises the children, while the man is out pursuing his career, is still very much with us. Anyone who believes that is not true should follow one of our top female seminary graduates from interview to interview as she tries to find a place to use her education in the church. Not only Roman Catholics and Southern Baptists discriminate against women in the church these days. The sad fact is that the Christian church which so insistently preaches the great commandment does not really want its women to love the Lord with their minds—at least not from pulpits. Let the women stay at home, volunteer in the Sunday school, work in the women's fellowship, and be content with love in their hearts and souls. As Harriet van Horne once remarked, "The most serious brain drain in the world is the drain in the kitchen sink. Down, down go the wit, the dreams, the talents of millions of women."

But consider also the role of males in our society. Men are still programmed in the United States to achieve. They are to get out there and do the job, solve the problem, seize the offensive, beat the competition. In short, the American male is supposed to set aside heart and soul in the competitive scramble for success. He is expected to exhaust himself in his job, at the expense of his marriage and children, and to have no qualms about uprooting his family if it means a promotion and higher salary.

The difficulty is, however, that something happens to this competitive male machine along about middle life. He suddenly realizes that he may never be number one in his company. Or having reached a position relatively near the top, he discovers that it is an empty location and that there is inside of him an aching void to feel and to love and to know the warmth of personal and emotional relationships. Sooner or later, the human soul grows homesick. The result is that many men look back to their homes and try to reintroduce themselves to their families, only to find that their families long ago learned how to live without them. Some men seek out new jobs, or new wives, or new love affairs, and we have the widespread phenomenon of middle-age divorce and remarriage. Perhaps, thinks the man, love and warmth can be found the second time around. But those are traits that are conditioned out of many men by competitive American society, and many of them find they no longer know how to express and exchange emotions. "You shall love the Lord your God with all your heart . . . and soul." American males, even in this time, need to hear first of all that they *have* hearts and souls and that the emotional and spiritual sides of their personalities are precious gifts of God, which are not to be sacrificed to the American economy or to the growth of their particular businesses.

But there is more to be said in relationship to this text. Both male and female in our society also need to hear the proclamation of the love of God that will make it possible for them to respond in answering love to God from the depth of their personalities. Consciousness-raising or sociological analyses or moralistic admonitions are really not going to make much of a dent in American economic practices. Our society is structured in such a way, and the roles of male and female are programmed in such a manner, that we may most efficiently keep the gross national product expanding. You do not change that state of affairs simply by criticizing it. You change it by prompting men and women to a love great enough to inspire them to live different lives. And such love can be prompted only by the story of the mercy of God.

Is it not finally when we see the love of God shining undimmed in the face of Jesus Christ that we know truly what we are meant to be and do? Is it not when his story has etched its sacrifice on our minds and hearts that we know we are made for more than Mammon and that then we are willing to trade our selfish

security for God's high adventure of love? Is it not
when Christ becomes the constant companion of our
days and years that we can cease to be conformed to
this world and can be persuaded and empowered to
give our whole persons as living sacrifices to his
goodly purpose? "Whom have I in heaven but thee?"
cries the psalmist. "And there is nothing upon earth
that I desire besides thee" (Ps. 73:25). Men and
women who share that faith can break the shackles of
our society's ways and truly love God with all their
hearts and souls and minds and strength. But it is not
possible to do so apart from knowing the love with
which God has first loved us.

Jeremiah 6:14

Let us briefly consider another text. In relation to
the conflict in our homes, we Christians need to pon-
der deeply the words of Jeremiah 6:14: "They have
healed the wound of my people lightly, saying 'Peace,
peace,' when there is no peace." Far too often Christian forgiveness and love have been turned into a su-
perficial veneer with which we have covered over marital conflicts and discord, pretending that all is well
between husband and wife when in truth almost nothing is well. We have this stereotype that Christian
families are always happy and laughing and loving.
And so our people are afraid to admit that they have
suppressed hostilities or that they bear inner grudges
and hatreds of one another that poison their spirits
daily. On this score, psychologists may be much wiser
than we, and some of them have made a career out of
teaching couples and families how to fight construc-
tively. But is that not what God is constantly doing in
his judgments upon us—fighting against us construc-
tively to make us whole again? Anger, conflict, judgment, wrath can be used in the process of salvation, as
God himself often uses them, and we Christian
preachers need to explore their uses from the Sunday

pulpit. What is in fact the nature of Christian forgiveness in the home? Can it ever be exercised when one feels superior to the other? Is it conditional upon a turning and a reform of conduct? Does it involve forgetfulness of the past, as if no wrong had been committed? When does a Christian mate call a spouse to account? And what is the time when the Christian spouse can legitimately abandon a marriage? Those are pressing questions for the people who sit out in front of us in the pews. Let us therefore not urge upon them, in our preaching, "Peace, peace," when they know no peace, healing their familial wounds lightly with clichés about supposed Christian love.

Family Life as a Source of Illustrations

These are just a few examples of how other passages from the scriptures can be used in relation to family life. But as every preacher knows, our homes are also a constant source of illustrations for other sermons, and examples taken from the life of the family can be used in sermons dealing with subjects other than those of the Christian home. By such use, the congregation is continually instructed in Christian family life, even while the preacher is treating other topics. Let me give just two examples that I have used elsewhere.

It is precisely through the instrument of our children that God often extends to us his forgiveness. Every parent has had the experience of unjustly punishing a child: we become tired and crotchety and whack a child on the behind, not so much because the child has been bad, but mostly to relieve our own feelings. What happens? Two minutes later, our child is hugging us and kissing us and saying, "I love you, Mommy," and in that instant we know we have been forgiven for our sinful past. The wrong we have done has not been held against us. It has been forgotten in love. We have the possibility of starting over, of making a new beginning. Through our children themselves, we are offered the healing of forgiveness.[1]

At our summer place . . . we live next door to a couple whose family has been split by a petty argument for four years. They got into a dispute with their brother and sister-in-law over who should clean the summer place. And now the relatives avoid one another and have never even seen each other's latest children. And that, good Christians, is the way of death and not the way of life. To love God means to forgive others as he has forgiven us.[2]

These illustrations were taken from my own experience, but one can also glean all sorts of family illustrations from others. There is this from Patrick Henry, in the eighteenth century, speaking of the legacy he left to his family:

I have now disposed of all my property to my family. There is one thing more I wish I could give them, and that is the Christian religion. If they had that, and I had not given them one shilling, they would have been rich; and if they had not that, and I had given them all the world, they would have been poor.

Or there is a clothing ad in *The New Yorker* that read, "Cricketeer. Because the quality of your clothes should be equal to the quality of your life." The preacher might comment that one wishes sometimes that the quality of our lives were equal to the quality of our clothes. Or one can use poems, such as this one from Gerard Manley Hopkins:

In the staring darkness
I can hear the harshness
Of the cold wind blowing.
I am warmly clad,
And I'm very glad
That I've got a home.[3]

Or there was this illustration, used in a sermon by George W. Truett, entitled "Why Do Souls Go Away from Jesus?":

> A U.S. senator explained to a skeptical colleague why he believed in the new birth: "My mother and my wife have both told me that they surrendered to Christ and have been born again, and they both live like it is so."[4]

The preacher also finds illustrations from family life by reading great literature. The character Creon in Sophocles' play *Antigone* speaks:

> For whoso rules his household worthily
> Will prove in civic matters no less wise.[5]

The preacher can collect such illustrations from many different sources. When they are used, they serve to illustrate not only that which is being preached but also the manner of Christians in their family life.

Two cautions need to be added, however. First, illustrations should always be brief, so that they do not take on a life of their own and divert attention from the main point of the sermon. Second, the preacher should resist the temptation repeatedly to use illustrations from his or her own home life.

It should also be pointed out that the use of such illustrations fosters a characteristic found in all good preaching—namely, specificity: the concrete application of texts to actual situations in our people's lives and, conversely, the illustration of the biblical message from specific situations in the home. One of the banes of the pulpit in our time is generality—telling our people to love God but never spelling out for them what that means in their everyday home life, urging them to lead Christian lives and never giving concrete shape to that in their mind's eye. Most of the persons in our congregations truly do want to live Christian lives. The difficulty is that so many of their preachers never picture for them just what the Christian way of life looks like.

A Sample Meditation: "Will You Honor Him?"

To give further illustration of how that can be done from the pulpit, let me reproduce here a brief meditation I delivered before the community of Union Theological Seminary in Virginia, during a fifteen-minute morning chapel service. The meditation deals with one portion of the Christian wedding vows.

Scripture Lesson: Romans 12:1–10, 21

In his letter to the Roman church, Paul has used eleven chapters to set forth the marvelous grace of God—to tell what God has done on behalf of humankind. Now here in chapter 12, he turns to our response to that grace. "Therefore, brethren," he writes (to paraphrase his words), "therefore I appeal to you by or in or through all of these mercies of God that I have written about, to present yourselves, your whole selves, as a living sacrifice, holy and acceptable to God, which is your reasonable service and response to what God has done for you." And part of that response, he says, is to "outdo one another in showing honor."

Honor. It is not a word we often use to describe the Christian life-style. Certainly it is a good Southern word. The University of Virginia has its honor code. Southern ladies and gentlemen have their sacred honor that must be defended and maintained at all costs. But in the Bible, the word is used somewhat differently, and it crops up again and again when the biblical writers are describing the life of faith. We all know we are to honor our fathers and our mothers. But there are also these statements: in Proverbs, "He who is kind to the needy honors him" (14:31); in Leviticus, "You shall rise up before the hoary head, and honor the face of an old man"

(19:32); in 1 Timothy, "honor widows" (5:3); in 1 Peter, "Honor all men; honor the emperor" (2:17).

It is this usage—this understanding of honor as a necessary part of the response of faith—that has passed into the traditional Christian marriage service. In that service, the woman is asked, "Will you have this man to be your husband; to live together in the covenant of marriage? Will you love him, comfort him, *honor* and keep him, in sickness and in health; and forsaking all others, be faithful to him as long as you both shall live?" So too to the man: "Will you love her, comfort her, *honor* and keep her . . . ?" Over that little word "honor" many a marriage has run aground in a storm and been battered to pieces against the rocks. And so perhaps it would be well for us to ask what it means for us to honor one another in our marriages. What does it mean in the Christian life, and so very practically, to honor your mate?

Let's start on the simplest level. To honor your mate in Christian marriage is to see that he or she is there. That may sound ludicrous to some of you newly married or newly engaged, for whom the whole world revolves around your beloved. But after a number of years, marriages have a way of settling down into a daily routine in which we no longer see one another. As Thornton Wilder put it in his play *Our Town*, "We don't have time to look at one another," especially when we are trying to run a parish or raise the children or get everything done here at the seminary. [The examples would be changed for a non-seminary congregation.] We don't have time to look at one another. The good-bye kiss at the door is forgotten, the greeting when one comes home is ignored. We never see that our mate looks tired or has cut a finger or has a lock of hair askew because he or she slept on it wrong last night. In fact, as a test, ask yourself what your mate was wearing when you left home this morning. In

Christian marriage, we have to see one another—
really look at each other—before there is any possibility of showing that honor we have promised.

Second, to honor one another in Christian marriage is to show one another courtesy. One of the
reasons the South is such a gracious place in which
to live is because its roots lie deep in the biblical
faith that considers courtesy—graciousness—a gift
of grace. And that graciousness, that courtesy, is to
be a mark of Christian marriage. We all perform
routine tasks for one another in our homes—mow-
ing the lawn, washing the dishes, cooking the supper, fetching a cup of coffee, holding open a door.
And after a while, those services come to be expected and taken for granted. But a "thank you"
occasionally for a routine service offered, an expression of gratitude or of pleasure, honors that service
and the person giving it. It says, "I appreciate what
you have done for me, and I appreciate you." I
sometimes think destructive jealousies arise in a
marriage because a mate shows more courtesy and
appreciation and thoughtfulness toward the person
next door or toward someone on the job than he or
she does toward the spouse at home.

Above all, to honor one another in Christian marriage means to esteem your mate. One of the biblical words for "honor" is the same as that for
"glory," and it has the same basic meaning:
"weight." Your mate is to have weight or esteem in
your eyes. He or she is to be seen as valuable, as
important, and not only for what the mate has ac-
complished but, above all, for who she or he is—a
person, fearfully and wonderfully made by God, ex-
pensively redeemed by Jesus Christ, a person with
hopes and fears and dreams and anxieties and abilities and shortcomings, a person living out a history
guided by God from an intricate past into an unknown future. To honor that person is to share all
that, to listen to it, to participate in it, to rejoice or

weep over it, apart from all censure or selfishness or superior comparisons with one's own life history. To honor your mate is to hold her or him esteemed in your eyes.

But it always and everywhere is also to make your mate esteemed in the eyes of others. I shall never forget a high school friend of mine who introduced her new husband to our community with the words, "Come, meet my husband. He's the fat one over there." The same lack of esteem is communicated, of course, when you talk about your mate's faults with a group of friends or family, or when you bawl out your mate in front of your mother or even in front of your children. Those are actions that debase, that degrade, that dishonor your mate in the eyes of others. And I suppose we do such things because we are fearful or prideful. We want to say, in so many words, "I am the superior one in this family," or we fear what Mother or our friends will think of our spouse, or we tear down the other in order to try to make ourselves look good. But the Gospel tells us that, as Christians, we have no need to justify ourselves any more, that perfect love casts out fear, and that Christ has delivered us from that pride which makes us think more highly of ourselves than we ought to think.

Esteem. Honor. Will you hold your mate in honor? Will you give him or her true worth and importance, not only in your eyes but in the eyes of all around you? Will you by word and action so cherish your marriage partner that he or she knows the quiet joy that comes with being loved and valued and considered important in another's eyes? This is what the Christian marriage vows ask of us when we take them.

We can fulfill those vows, of course, only by the grace of God. But the grace, the power of God to lead a Christian life has been given. Paul, and indeed all of the New Testament, shouts out that the power has been given—lent to us by the mercies of God through Jesus Christ our Lord. Therefore I appeal to you, by those mercies, to present yourselves as a living sacrifice, holy and acceptable to God. "Let love be genuine; hate what is evil, hold fast to what is good." And in your marriages, "outdo one another in showing honor."

7

Constructing the Sermon

Most of the preachers who read this book will have some time ago settled on their own particular method of sermon construction. We each have our own style and our own way of going about the homiletical task, and there is not much profit in one preacher trying to impose his or her method on another. Above all, there is no profit in using someone else's sermon outline. That is a dishonest endeavor that prevents the preacher ever from making the biblical text his or her own, and were it up to me I would consign every book of sermon outlines ever published to the trash heap. No one of us can preach the Word of God unless that Word has first been absorbed into our own heart and mind and become like Jeremiah's fire, burning in our bones and impelling us to deliver it (Jer. 20:9).

Nevertheless, as one surveys the preaching being carried on in the United States, one is impressed by certain characteristics that have crept into American preaching and that, if discarded, would greatly strengthen the message being proclaimed from the church's pulpits.

First is the tendency among so many preachers to ignore the biblical text. One gets the impression that the chosen scripture lesson for the day has been studied only long enough for the preacher to get a "sermon idea" from it. The scripture passage is then left behind, and the preacher launches forth into a development of the "idea," elaborating on it by use of personal opinion or current thought and practice. Or, very often in our time, the preacher will impose the ideology of some contemporary group or cause on the text and end up preaching the standard views of the "liberals" or "conservatives," "feminists" or "gays," "pro-lifers" or "pro-abortionists," "peace activists" or "racial-ethnic advocates." One-issue preachers and ideologues are a curse of our time, imposing their narrow views on the scriptures and fragmenting gospel and church, and all preachers should ask themselves if they have fallen captive to some ideology or if they have in fact preserved the freedom of the Word from the world. To be sure, all of us are influenced in the way we read the scriptures by the situation and society in which we live, but the preacher should use every scholarly tool at his or her disposal to try truly to hear the message of the text, in its immediate and total canonical context.

For example, a negligent preacher might use the text of Malachi 2:16, "I hate divorce," with no regard to its context in verses 10–16. But the whole passage concerns divorce and remarriage with foreign women by the men of post-exilic Judah (v. 11), easy idolatry of those foreign women's deities (v. 11), the unique role that Judah was supposed to play as the Lord's covenant people (v. 10), and God's resulting attitude: Because of such covenant violation, the Lord will no longer accept Judah's worship (v. 13). The passage is a good deal more complicated than an isolated use of verse 16 would make it appear, and divorce, in the passage, is set in the centuries-long context of Judah's role as God's covenant people. So too a discussion of divorce in our time would similarly have to be placed in that context and its relation to the service and worship of the new covenant people in the church explicated. There is no substitute in preaching for the immersion of the preacher in the text.

Second, when one looks at the product of the pulpit in this country, one is impressed by how many sermons are little more than moralistic exhortations. So many preachers are proclaiming the law and not the Gospel! A text is chosen—for example, "You shall love your neighbor as yourself" (Mark 12:31)—and applied to the marital relation, as we have earlier discussed. But then the sermon consists in little more than admonitions to follow the command. "You should," "we need to," "we must," "you ought"—those are the words that pepper the sermon, and the Gospel is turned into an exhortation to follow the law of the Bible.

To be sure, the law has an important place in the Gospel, as we have pointed out. It convicts us, it converts us, and it guides us in the Christian life. (For example, Christians cannot feel good ever again about hating anyone!) But the difficulty is that such preaching ignores the fact that we, by our own power, are impotent to follow the law. "I can will what is right, but I cannot do it" because I live under the power of sin (Rom. 7:18). The law, which so many preachers promise their congregations will give them life, proves simply to convict and give them death instead (Rom. 7:10). Our people want to love and find they cannot do so, and they end up frustrated, angry, guilty, some times rejecting forever a message that promises them hope but that leaves them in despair.

The Gospel alone makes it possible to follow our Lord's commands, and every sermon that exhorts the congregation to a course of action must at the same time proclaim that action of God by which alone power is given to be obedient. Only if God in Christ pours his love into our hearts by the activity of his Spirit do we have the power to love. Only if God gives the Spirit of forgiveness do we have the ability to forgive one another. Only if God inspires goodwill in us do we have the willpower to do the good. "Love, joy, peace, patience, kindness, goodness, faithfulness,

gentleness, self-control"—these are the fruits of the
Spirit, says Paul (Gal. 5:22–23), not the fruits of our
sinful natures, and every sermon must offer that Spirit
by which such fruits are produced. In other words, the
sermon must talk about God—about his action, about
what he has done in the past and what he is doing in
the present and future, about his character, his desire
and will and purpose. For when a sermon talks about
God, as he is revealed to us through the scriptures,
God himself in Christ through the Spirit draws near to
us and dwells in our hearts, and we are given the
power to walk in his ways and to obey his commandments. That is the reason why any sermon that does
not grow out of the biblical Word is powerless; only
God's Word works in our hearts to transform our
lives. But that is also the reason why any sermon that
is made up of moralistic exhortation alone is useless.

At the same time, and in the third place, there is no
doubt that human will plays a large part in the recep-
tion and implementation of God's will in our lives. We
must in fact "work out [our] own salvation with fear
and trembling" (Phil. 2:12). God alone can transform
our lives, but we must open ourselves to that transfor-
mation and by the most strenuous faith approve and
appropriate it as our own. It therefore follows that
sermons which seek to bring about change in a congregation's life must furnish the motivation for wanting that change. There are so many sermons delivered
in our churches which urge upon the people in the
pews the Christian way of life and yet which give no
reason whatsoever for wanting that life. We tell our
people they should be joyful but proclaim to them no
reason for joy. We exhort them to trust God but spell
out no bases for that trust. We urge them to follow
some command but give them no reasons why they
should do so. And so our people are left with no motivation for that strenuous exercise of the will to which
the Christian faith calls them.

The result is that our people are very likely to remain as they are. Why should a woman give up some habit with which she has been comfortable? Why should a man discard convictions he has held all his life? Why adopt new views, new life-style, new character, new goals when the old have served so well and have allowed one to exist in society with at least a modicum of success? Why indeed?—unless there is a pearl of great price that is more valuable than anything else in this world; unless there is joy to be had in a treasure whose worth never diminishes; unless all the little satisfactions and successes of this world cannot begin to compare to a present company with God and to the glories of a future he has planned for those who love him; unless God himself is so lovable, so wise, so tender and compassionate in his comfort, so never-failing in his loyalty, that to miss companionship with him is to miss life itself; unless to be fully human is to live with Christ and to die in him is gain. If those things be true, along with so many more from the Gospel, then indeed a person may want to be a Christian. And every sermon should be framed in such manner that it calls forth that desire.

Fourth, there also seems to be a problem in our time with achieving proper balance in our sermons. So much of their content is made up of gloomy pictures of all our problems! We preachers are very good at analyzing what is wrong with our society, and we dwell on that wrong at such length that we spend very little time delivering the good news. Part of that is due to our pride, of course—we imagine we are modern-day prophets, "filled with power, with the Spirit of the Lord, and with justice and might, to declare to Jacob his transgression and to Israel his sin" (Micah 3:8). We are the champions of justice and righteousness in our society, we imagine, and our people need to be told just how unjust and unrighteous they are.

To be sure, the prophetic message of judgment needs always to be delivered, lest we become a society "thickening upon [its] lees," whose citizens say "in their hearts, 'The LORD will not do good, nor will he do ill' " (Zeph. 1:12). But we preachers need also to remember that the biblical message of judgment was always an integral part of God's act of salvation: God judges in order to save. And when the new age of salvation has begun (as it has in the person of Jesus Christ), to dwell on the wrong to the exclusion of God's right is to leave our people without the truth and therefore without hope. A twelve-year-old can tell what is wrong with our society, but it takes a preacher to proclaim how God is setting it right, and we seem to have become inept in our time at spelling out in full the good news. Surely the bulk of the sermon should be occupied with the details of that gospel—with all God has done in Jesus Christ and with what that means for our living. Then our congregations will be able to live in hope and joy, in the midst of our hopeless and cynical society. "The opposite of a Christian people," wrote George Bernanos, "is a people grown sad and old."[1] The task of us heralds of good news is to proclaim the message that will rescue them from that situation.

Alongside that, however, in the fifth place, the sermon must be careful to avoid that triumphalism that sings with Robert Browning's Pippa that "God's in his heaven—all's right with the world." The kingdom has not yet come on earth even as it is in heaven, and every soul who sits in front of us in the pew is undergoing some sort of suffering; the richest, most comfortable, most intelligent, most healthy, even the most faithful among them is undergoing some sort of suffering. The New Testament knows that though nothing can separate us from the love of Christ, we still have to make our way through this wicked world. "As it is," says Hebrews (2:8), "we do not yet see everything in subjection to [God]. But we see Jesus. . . ." That is "as it is"; that is the state of the world. And in announcing the good news, we have to be careful not to overlook the bad. I sometimes think that the best compliment any preacher can receive is to have some parishioner say after the sermon, "You told it like it is," because that means the reality of that parishioner's life has been set in relation to the gospel. His or her sin has not been overlooked, but neither has it been exaggerated; the suffering has been acknowledged in all its reality; God's sure victory in Christ has been announced, but the battles still to be fought have been portrayed; and Christ has been proclaimed as Commander and Sustainer in every engagement. "We do not yet see everything in subjection to [God]. But we see Jesus" (Heb. 2:8–9). That is the realism of the Christian pulpit.

With all these points in mind, let us finally say a few words about the mechanics of constructing the sermon. The most difficult task, of course, is moving from the text to the sermon—making that hermeneutical leap from the "then" of the Bible to the "now" of the congregation. In bridging that gap many preachers go awry, because they do not know how validly to apply the text to the lives of their people.

Such a hermeneutical move may be made, first of all, by comparing the situation of the people of God in the text with the situation of the congregation. Are the two in any way analogous from a historical point of view? But above all, are those two situations similar or analogous in respect to the relationship of the people to God?

Very often, few comparisons can be drawn between the text's historical setting and our own—the world of the Bible and our twentieth-century world are two very different realities, and the preacher must never forget that enormous historical difference; time and distance cannot simply be telescoped. Similarly, the preacher must remember that the text is dealing with the covenant people and not with a pluralistic nation; thus the proper modern parallel to biblical Israel is not the United States or any other nation—not even the modern Israeli state—but the new covenant peo-

ple found in the church and among the faithful
throughout the world. That group—the covenant people of God—forms the subject of all analogies drawn
between the text's "then" and the present's "now."
And the preacher will find his or her most pregnant
opportunities for drawing comparisons by asking after
the situation before God. Is Israel's or the early
church's situation before God in the text analogous to
our situation before him in the church? That question
prompts the sparks to fly.

For example, is Israel's relation to God in Malachi
2:10–16 analogous to our relation to God in the
church? Does God refuse to accept also our prayers
and worship because of our faithlessness in our marriages? What bearing does God's subsequent act in
Jesus Christ have on the Malachi text? And what, then,
are the implications for our lives as individuals and as
members of the church? Out of questions such as
these the stuff of biblical sermons grows.

The use of analogy between the text's situation before God and our own is the principal hermeneutical
tool in applying the biblical text to the life of the
congregation, because we stand in continuity with the
covenant people and therefore are dealing with the
same God. But it may be that the text should be applied to a congregation on the basis of fulfillment instead. The Bible is full of promises—of judgment and
of salvation—and it may be that the congregation is
the heir of the fulfillment of one of those promises.
For example, as we have earlier pointed out, Jesus'
promise that whoever loses his life shall save it and
whoever saves his life shall lose it certainly finds its
confirmation in the relationships of the home. Only as
spouses give themselves away to one another in total
commitment are they given the freedom and joy of
Christian marriage. Only as parents lose themselves in
bringing up their children in "the nurture and admonition of the Lord" are they rewarded with children
grown up into responsible and loving human beings.

God's promises, given to us in the scriptures, are fulfilled in Christian lives time and again because God is faithful, and that may be the hermeneutical approach dictated by the text.

In seeking the valid application of the text to the present, the preacher has always to be careful to avoid the allegorization and psychologizing and sentimentalizing of the biblical message that are heard so often from the pulpit.

Having decided on the hermeneutical method of application, the preacher then has the task of engaging in what Leander Keck has called "priestly listening"[2]—that is, listening to the text on behalf of the congregation. And at this stage of sermon construction, all sorts of questions should be asked: How will my congregation hear this biblical passage? Are there portions of it—words, concepts, views of God and human beings—that they will not understand and that therefore should be explained? Are there portions of the passage that my people will reject out of hand, because of presuppositions and customs that they have, and, if so, how will I avoid that rejection or turn it into acceptance of the biblical message? What are the contrasts between the text's views of a faithful life and the views held in our society? What are the similarities? Are most of my people living by the truth of this passage, or have they left it behind? What does the text affirm in my congregation's living and what does it call into question? What response should my people have to this Word of God? How will I move them toward that response? What motivation will best inspire them to make the biblical Word their own and thereby to be faithful to God?

The answers to these questions and many others like them form that homiletical dialogue whereby the preacher sets the biblical text in conversation with the congregation. But it should be emphasized that the preacher is conversing with the text on behalf of his or her people and therefore deals with the text in terms of their lives and not simply in terms of his or her own life. For example, the preacher in his or her own marriage may be able joyfully to affirm that marriage is a symbol of Christ's relation with his church, as stated in Ephesians 5:32. But that may seem like utter nonsense to some persons in the pews, and it is with the latter's views and not the preacher's that the sermon has to deal, or it will never bring home the message of the gospel to their hearts. Sermons therefore are not made up primarily of the preacher's own personal testimony but are, rather, the preacher's wrestling with a text in the congregation's stead. We listen to the Word of God with our people's ears; we are bound up in the bundle of life with them. And we clarify, think through, struggle with, explain, make desirable and true and joyful the Word of God on their behalf and in relationship to their actual lives.

Paul did that in his preaching. "I have become all things to all men," he wrote, "that I might by all means save some" (1 Cor. 9:22). But by that statement, Paul did not mean that he gave up his gospel and Christian life and adopted others' positions and life-styles. No, "I am free," he said, but "I have made myself a slave to all, that I might win the more" (v. 19). Not under the law himself, he became as one under the law (v. 20). Not being outside the law of Christ, he nevertheless became as one outside the law (v. 21). Not being weak but living in the power of Christ, he did however become weak (v. 22). In short, Paul identified completely with his hearers and thought their thoughts and entered into their lives and their reactions as he preached to them "Jesus Christ and him crucified" (2:2). He did it "all for the sake of the gospel," he said (9:23), because, more than anything else, he desired that the Gospel prosper until all shared in its good news.

We preachers have the same calling—to proclaim Jesus Christ and him crucified until all bless his name and every knee bows and every tongue confesses that he is Lord of their lives. And so to every parishioner sitting out there in front of us on Sunday morning—to every divorced, every married, every single, every widowed, every young, and every old person—to every suffering or celebrating soul, we proclaim the gospel of God in his Son, because that gospel means life for our loved people in their homes, and joy, and the peace of God.

Notes

Chapter 2: The Social Context and Its Impact

1. These statistics and others that follow are taken from U.S. Census Bureau figures.

2. *Newsweek*, February 11, 1980, p. 58.

3. Ibid., p. 63.

4. Ibid., p. 58.

5. "Divorce court lets children be heard" by Ron Russell, the *Detroit News*. Quoted in the *Richmond Times-Dispatch*, May 22, 1986.

6. Quoted in "Teens found to hide divorce anguish" by Betty Booker, *Richmond Times-Dispatch*, March 10, 1986.

7. "Young adults describe anguish when their parents separate" by Georgia Dullea, New York Times Service. Quoted in the *Richmond Times-Dispatch*, November 24, 1985.

8. " 'Married,' 'mother,' sound as brave as 'single,' " *Richmond Times-Dispatch*, March 30, 1986, p. H-6.

9. *Time*, December 9, 1985, p. 79.

Chapter 3: Dealing with Basic Presuppositions

1. *Newsweek*, October 15, 1979, p. 140.

2. "Unrealistic love ideals misleading," Associated Press, *Richmond Times-Dispatch*, 1986.

3. *Newsweek*, October 15, 1979, p. 140.

4. Quoted in "Women Urged to Weigh Options" by

Robin Traywick, *Richmond Times-Dispatch,* February 4, 1980, p. A-6.

5. Quoted in " 'Healthy family' depends on couple" by Betty Booker, *Richmond Times-Dispatch,* March 20, 1983, p. H-10.

Chapter 4: What Does the Bible Say?

1. Starhawk, *The Spiral Dance: A Rebirth of the Ancient Religion of the Great Goddess* (San Francisco: Harper & Row, 1979), p. 196.
2. Serena Vassady.
3. Quoted in the *Richmond Times-Dispatch,* January 1, 1981, p. D-4.
4. Ibid.
5. Serena Vassady.

Chapter 5: Speaking the Truth in Love

1. T. S. Eliot, *The Family Reunion* (London: Faber & Faber, 1939), p. 97.
2. Betty Booker, loc. cit. ch. 3, note 5.
3. "The Blessed Virgin Compared to the Air We Breathe," lines 34–36, Gerard Manley Hopkins, *Poems and Prose of Gerard Manley Hopkins,* selected and with an introduction and notes by W. H. Gardner (Penguin Books, 1978), p. 55.

Chapter 6: Using Other Texts and Illustrations

1. Elizabeth Achtemeier, *The Committed Marriage* (Philadelphia: Westminster Press, 1976), pp. 197–198.
2. Elizabeth Achtemeier, *Preaching as Theology and Art* (Nashville: Abingdon Press, 1984), p. 111.
3. *The Poems of Gerard Manley Hopkins,* 4th ed., ed. by W. H. Gardner and N. H. MacKenzie (London: Oxford University Press, 1967), p. 172.
4. Quoted in *The Twentieth Century Pulpit,* ed. by James W.

Cox and Patricia Cox (Nashville: Abingdon Press, 1981), p 260.

5. Sophocles, *Antigone,* lines 661–662, trans. by F. Storr, Loeb Classical Library (Cambridge, Mass.: Harvard University Press).

Chapter 7: Constructing the Sermon

1. George Bernanos, *The Diary of a Country Priest,* trans. from the French by Pamela Morris (Garden City, N.Y.: Image Books, 1974), p. 14.

2. Leander Keck, *The Bible in the Pulpit: The Renewal of Biblical Preaching* (Nashville· Abingdon Press, 1978).

Suggested Reading

Achtemeier, Elizabeth. *The Committed Marriage.* Biblical Perspectives on Current Issues. Philadelphia: Westminster Press, 1976.

Anderson, Douglas. *New Approaches to Family Pastoral Care.* Philadelphia: Fortress Press, 1980.

Arnold, William V., et al. *Divorce: Prevention or Survival.* Philadelphia: Westminster Press, 1977.

————. *When Your Parents Divorce.* Christian Care Book. Philadelphia: Westminster Press, 1980.

Bach, George, and Peter Wyden. *The Intimate Enemy: How to Fight Fair in Love and Marriage.* New York: Avon Books, 1969.

Clinebell, Charlotte. *Meet Me in the Middle.* New York: Harper & Row, 1970.

———— and Howard Clinebell. *The Intimate Marriage.* New York: Harper & Row, 1970.

Gardner, Richard. *The Boys and Girls' Book About Divorce.* New York: Science House, 1970.

Hoster, Helen K. *To Love Again: Remarriage for the Christian.* Nashville: Abingdon Press, 1985.

Hunt, Joan, and Richard Hunt. *Preparing for Christian Marriage: Couples.* Nashville: Abingdon Press, 1981.

Mace, David, and Vera Mace. *Men, Women, and God.* Atlanta: John Knox Press, 1976.

————. *What's Happening to Clergy Marriages?* Nashville: Abingdon Press, 1980.

Oates, Wayne E., and Wade Rowatt. *Before You Marry Them: Guidebook for Pastors.* Nashville: Broadman Press, 1976.

Rice, F. Philip. *Contemporary Marriage.* Boston: Allyn & Bacon, 1983.

————. *Morality and Youth.* Philadelphia: Westminster Press, 1980.

————. *Stepparenting.* Westport, Conn.: Condor Publishing Co., 1979.

————. *The Working Mother's Guide to Child Development.* Englewood Cliffs, N.J.: Prentice-Hall, 1979.

Sawyers, Lindell, ed. *Faith and Families.* Philadelphia: Geneva Press, 1986.

Terrien, Samuel. *Till the Heart Sings: A Biblical Theology of Manhood and Womanhood.* Philadelphia: Fortress Press, 1985.

Thatcher, Floyd W., and Harriet Thatcher. *Long-term Marriage.* Waco, Tex.: Word Books, 1980.

Wynn, John Charles. *Family Therapy in Pastoral Ministry.* New York: Harper & Row, 1982.

DATE DUE

MAR 15 '89			